Vampire to The Lady of Fátima

PSYCHOLOGY OF HISTORY'S GREAT FEARS

Dr. Robin K Mathew

Writer's Pocket

First published by Writer's Pocket in 2026

email: editor@writerspocket.com

Cover Design by Dr Robin K Mathew

ISBN-13: 978-93-7248-814-2

www.writerspocket.com

CONTENTS

PREFACE

History is often presented as a clean sequence of dates, rulers, and decisive moments. Yet beneath that orderly surface lie events that feel unsettling, absurd, or deeply disturbing—moments when reality itself seems to bend. This book gathers such stories, not as myths or fantasies, but as documented episodes where the ordinary world briefly gave way to something far stranger.

This is not a book that asks you to choose between science and belief. Instead, it invites you to stand where they meet. Many of these events can be examined through psychology, neuroscience, or social behavior.

At its heart, this book is about vulnerability. It shows how hunger, stress, power, belief, and misunderstanding can reshape minds and societies, sometimes with irreversible consequences. It also reminds us that behind every strange event is a human experience—confused, frightened, hopeful, or desperate to survive.

Dr. Robin K Mathew

Chapter 1

Vampire in Sacramento

"The greatest tragedy of the mind is not that it breaks, but that it breaks in silence." — Carl Jung

A Man, Not a Myth

Come closer and listen with care. This is not a story born from superstition or horror fiction. It is a true account of how a human mind, deeply wounded and left untreated, slowly lost its grip on reality and turned fear into violence.

His name was Richard Trenton Chase. History remembers him by a chilling title: *the Vampire of Sacramento.* The name sounds unreal, almost theatrical, but the man behind it was painfully real. His story is often cited when discussing clinical vampirism, a rare and extreme psychological condition in which a person believes they must consume blood in order to stay alive.

Richard Chase was not born a monster. He was born in California in 1950, into a home marked by instability and emotional neglect. His father was cruel and abusive. His mother struggled with serious mental illness and long-standing depression. Love, safety, and emotional grounding were absent. From early childhood, Richard lived inside loneliness. He grew quiet, withdrawn, and deeply isolated, carrying sadness that had nowhere to go.

The Slow Fracture of Reality

As Richard grew older, the cracks in his inner world widened. Psychologists later noted that his childhood showed patterns associated with deep emotional disturbance, often referred to as the Macdonald Triad—persistent bedwetting beyond early childhood, cruelty to animals, and fire-setting. These behaviors do not cause violence on their own, but they often signal a child in severe psychological distress.

By his early twenties, Richard's mind began to drift further from reality. He developed powerful somatic delusions, believing that something was terribly wrong with his body. He became convinced that his blood was turning to dust, that his heart was shrinking, that his organs had been stolen, and that his skull was breaking apart. These were not passing thoughts. To him, they were undeniable facts.

Out of these delusions emerged one terrifying belief: he would die unless he drank blood. This idea settled into his mind with complete certainty. It was not desire or curiosity. It was survival.

Blood as Salvation

At first, Richard turned to animals. He hunted dogs, cats, birds, and small creatures. He killed them and drank their blood, sometimes storing remains in containers. On some occasions, he injected blood directly into his own body, convinced it would restore him. To an outside observer, these acts were horrifying. To Richard, they were medicine.

Eventually, he was admitted to a psychiatric hospital. Doctors noticed blood around his mouth. When questioned, he gave vague explanations, once claiming it was from shaving. His medical records were clear and alarming. They described a man suffering from intense delusions, especially the belief that his blood was disintegrating and that unseen forces were trying to kill him.

The illness was recognized. It was documented. And yet, it was disastrously underestimated.

After a short period, hospital staff believed Richard had improved. His medication was stopped. He was released. But his delusions had never disappeared. They had only retreated into silence. Once free, they returned stronger than before. He became convinced that an alien presence was draining his blood and that only blood consumption could save him.

When Fear Became Violence

Soon, Richard began entering homes. At first, he killed animals inside them. Then, his fear crossed a final boundary. He began killing people. The pattern was chillingly consistent: murder, consumption of blood, sometimes injection, collecting remains, and acts of necrophilia. These were not acts of rage or pleasure. In his mind, they were acts of survival.

In 1979, Richard Trenton Chase was convicted of six murders. During the trial, something deeply unsettling became clear. He showed no guilt. He expressed no fear. When a psychiatrist asked whether he felt remorse, Richard answered calmly, *"Why? Wouldn't I have died if I hadn't done that?"*

His answer revealed the depth of his illness. He did not see himself as a killer. He saw himself as someone who had narrowly escaped death.

The Law and the Broken Mind

To understand how the court viewed him, one must understand the M'Naghten Rules, a legal standard developed in 1843. These rules state that a person may be found legally insane if mental illness made them incapable of understanding what they were doing, or incapable of knowing that it was wrong.

Richard Chase lived in a world where reality had collapsed. His actions were guided not by choice, but by terror-driven belief. Yet the law could not fully reconcile his illness with the harm he caused.

An Ending Without Peace

In prison, his delusions continued. He refused food and water, believing they were poisoned. His mind remained trapped in fear. In 1980, while on death row at San Quentin State Prison, Richard Trenton Chase took his own life. Even at the end, the illness did not release him.

And so this story closes not with resolution, but with a warning.

Mental illness does not announce itself as evil. It begins quietly, as fear, confusion, and pain. When ignored, misunderstood, or left untreated, it can grow into something devastating.

Richard Chase was not born a monster. He was a man whose mind, in trying desperately to save itself, lost the ability to know what saving truly meant.

Chapter 2

The Green Children of Woolpit

"The most mysterious things are not those that come from another world, but those that come from human suffering we do not yet understand." — Michel de Montaigne

A Quiet Village, an Unquiet Day

Listen gently. This story comes from a distant century, when life moved slowly and wonder lived close to fear.

It was the twelfth century, in Woolpit, a small farming village in Suffolk, England. The name itself came from the deep pits dug around the fields to trap wolves. The land was flat and open. People rose with the sun, worked the soil, and measured time by bells and seasons. Nothing unexpected ever came to Woolpit.

Until one afternoon, something did happen.

From one of the wolf pits near the fields, villagers heard strange sounds—soft cries, murmurs unlike any language they knew. When they gathered around and looked down, what they saw unsettled them deeply.

Two children had climbed out of the pit. A boy and a girl.

They were small, frightened, and clearly exhausted. But it was not their fear that froze the villagers in place. It was their skin.

It was green.

Not painted. Not stained. A pale, living green, as if it belonged to them.

Children from Nowhere

The children wore clothes no one recognized—neither English nor foreign in any familiar way. When spoken to, they did not understand a single word. Their speech was musical but strange, unlike any tongue heard in the region.

The villagers brought them food. Bread, meat, milk, cooked vegetables. The children refused everything. Only when raw beans were offered did they eat, and even then with desperation, as though they had been starving.

Fear grew quietly. Some villagers wondered if the children had come from a distant land beyond known maps. Others whispered darker ideas—that they were beings from beneath the earth, or from somewhere not meant for humans at all.

The boy was weak. Within days, he fell ill and died.

The girl survived.

The Girl Who Stayed

Time passed. Slowly, the girl learned English. At first her words were broken, fragile. But she persisted. As she grew stronger, she began to eat ordinary food—cooked vegetables, fish, bread.

And as her body healed, something remarkable happened.

The green color of her skin began to fade.

Little by little, it disappeared, until she looked like any other young woman in the village.

When she could finally speak clearly, the villagers asked what they had waited so long to know.

Where did you come from?

Her answer was simple, and strange.

She said she and her brother came from a land where everyone was green. A place with no bright sun, only a dim, constant light. One day, while tending animals, they heard the sound of a bell. Drawn to it, they followed the sound until a sudden brightness overwhelmed them. Blinded and frightened, they wandered until they fell into the pit. That was all she remembered.

No one could prove her story false. No one could prove it true.

She grew up in Woolpit, worked, lived quietly, and eventually married. But the mystery of her arrival never left the village.

A Modern Look at an Old Mystery

Centuries later, doctors and historians returned to the tale, not with fear, but with science.

They suggested a simple, human explanation.

The green color may have come from severe iron deficiency, a condition once known as *chlorosis* and now understood as hypochromic anemia. In malnourished children, this illness can cause weakness, confusion, poor growth, and a pale or greenish tint to the skin.

Why the strange language? The children may have come from an isolated rural community, speaking a dialect unknown to the villagers.

Why only beans? Beans may have been the only food they recognized, or the only food their weakened bodies could tolerate.

When the girl began eating a balanced diet, her iron levels recovered. Her strength returned. And the green faded away.

What the Story Leaves Us

There may have been no hidden world beneath the earth. No magic. No visitors from beyond.

Only two children, lost, starving, and ill—carrying the marks of hunger on their skin.

And so, the story of the Green Children of Woolpit remains, not as a tale of the supernatural, but as a quiet reminder:

That the human body, when pushed to the edge of survival, can appear mysterious.

That fear often grows where understanding is absent. And that some legends are born not from wonder, but from compassion arriving too late.

Chapter 3

The Cadaver Synod

"Hatred is gained as much by good works as by evil."
— Niccolò Machiavelli

A Church Consumed by Power

History sometimes records events so disturbing that they feel unreal, as though they belong to a fever dream rather than the past. The Cadaver Synod is one such moment. It took place not in a battlefield or a dark alley, but inside the Vatican itself—in the year 897, at the very heart of Western Christianity.

This was a violent age. Rome was not guided by faith alone, but torn apart by rival noble families, shifting alliances, and constant fear. The papacy was less a spiritual office and more a prize to be seized. Popes rose and fell quickly, often dragged down by politics rather than doctrine. Power did not rest easily, and revenge waited patiently.

A Pope Who Left Enemies Behind

Pope Formosus ruled from 891 until his death in 896. His reign was troubled from the beginning. He involved himself deeply in European power struggles, choosing sides between kings and emperors, backing rulers who later fell, and turning against those who once supported him. Each decision carved new enemies.

When Formosus died, his body was buried. The prayers were said. The rituals were completed. By all reason, his story should have ended there.

But hatred does not always end with death.

The Order That Shocked Rome

Formosus's successor, Pope Stephen VI, carried a bitterness that had not cooled with time. Less than a year after Formosus's burial, Stephen issued an order so grotesque that even hardened soldiers recoiled.

He demanded that Formosus be put on trial.

The guards protested. The man had been dead for nine months. His body was decaying in the grave.

Stephen's answer was cold and absolute: the body still existed. And that was enough.

A Trial Without a Voice

Under cover of darkness, the grave was opened. The corpse of Pope Formosus was pulled from the earth and dressed again in full papal robes. His body, stiff and collapsing, was carried into the Lateran Basilica and placed on a throne meant for the living head of the Church.

Servants had to prop the body upright when it fell forward.

Then the trial began.

Stephen VI stood before the corpse and screamed accusations at it. He charged the dead pope with breaking Church law, betraying alliances, and unlawfully holding office. Each word was soaked in fury.

To preserve the appearance of justice, a terrified deacon was forced to act as Formosus's defense lawyer. He spoke on behalf of a body that could not hear him, could not respond, and could not even exist in the way the court pretended it did.

The verdict had already been decided.

Formosus was declared guilty.

His papacy was erased. All his acts were declared null. It was as though he had never ruled at all.

Punishing the Dead

The cruelty did not end with words.

The robes were stripped from the corpse. The fingers that had once given blessings were cut off. The body was dragged through the streets of Rome while people watched in horrified silence. No one dared to speak.

At last, the corpse was thrown into the Tiber River, as if Rome itself were trying to wash away a memory it could no longer bear.

When Fear Turns Back on Power

The city did not find peace.

Stories spread that the river had returned Formosus's body to shore, as though even nature rejected the crime. Whether true or not, the tale took hold of the public imagination. Fear turned into anger. Anger turned into revolt.

Within months, Stephen VI was arrested. One night, alone in his prison cell, he was strangled to death.

The next pope reversed everything Stephen had done. Formosus was buried again, this time with full honors. The Church tried to move on.

But history did not forget.

What the Cadaver Synod Reveals

The Cadaver Synod was not madness alone. It was political terror, carefully staged. By humiliating a dead pope, Stephen VI sent a clear message to the living: no one was beyond his reach—not even memory itself.

In a time poisoned by instability, paranoia, and violence, power sought to control not only the present, but the past. When fear hardens into hatred, even sacred spaces can become theaters of cruelty.

Chapter 4

The Unseen Economics of Lust

"Where there is desire, there is a market." — Adam Smith

The Older Pattern

This story does not begin with a website, a subscription page, or a payment button. It begins much earlier, with a quiet and persistent pattern in human behavior.

Across cultures and studies, one truth has remained steady for decades: men consume sexual content far more than women. Research shows that men who use pornography frequently often speak of loneliness, insecurity, and dissatisfaction with their bodies and sex lives. Desire, in these cases, is rarely only physical. It is tied to something deeper—a need to be noticed, to feel valued, to escape isolation, even if only for a moment.

The digital age did not create this hunger. It simply learned how to measure it, package it, and sell it.

A New Marketplace

As the internet evolved, a new marketplace took shape—one where attention, intimacy, and fantasy could be exchanged directly, without gatekeepers. In this space, a clear imbalance appeared.

Men arrived mostly as consumers. Women emerged largely as creators.

This shift quietly redefined how desire moved through the economy.

Architecture of Desire

Nowhere is this divide more visible than on OnlyFans. In 2023, the platform processed more than $6.6 billion. About 70 percent of its creators were women, while the overwhelming majority of paying users were men. The system favored the seller: 80 percent of every dollar spent went straight to the creator.

Yet the rewards were uneven.

Most creators earned modest amounts, roughly $150 to $180 per month. A small minority, however, rose far above the rest. Like many digital platforms, OnlyFans followed a steep power curve. The top 1 percent of creators earned nearly one-third of all revenue, while the top 10 percent captured around 73 to 75 percent. Many of these top earners were women who transformed male desire into multi-million-dollar businesses.

The Turn Toward Obsession

Subscriptions were only the starting point. As competition intensified, creators discovered that the real profits did not come from mass appeal, but from obsession—from superfans and from niches so specific and personal that traditional adult platforms could not serve them.

This marked a sharp turn in the economy of desire.

When the Body Becomes the Product

Some creators sold life-size silicone replicas of themselves, shipped in coffin-style boxes and dressed in their own worn underwear. Others sold bodily fluids—bottled breast milk, urine jars priced at $71 for 150 milliliters, and used menstrual products selling for $40 to $100. Some gained attention by selling fart jars, later converted into NFTs. Others went further, offering poop jars and custom scat-themed videos.

In the age of social media, desire no longer lived only in imagination or behind private screens. It became measurable, marketable, and at times deeply strange.

Across platforms such as OnlyFans, Twitter, Reddit, Etsy, and niche fetish marketplaces, a growing trade emerged around sex-adjacent products that went far beyond traditional adult content. These were not explicit acts, but physical traces of the body itself—fluids, clippings, byproducts, and personal remnants—packaged, priced, and sold to buyers who wanted something more intimate than images or videos.

Icons of Commodification

Some of the most well-known examples came from social-media figures who turned notoriety into strategy.

Belle Delphine sold a 1:1 silicone sex doll, shipped in a coffin-style box and dressed in her own underwear. Earlier, she had sold "GamerGirl Bath Water"—500-milliliter jars of used bath water priced at $30 each. The first batch sold out in three days and reportedly earned around $18,000. The water itself was irrelevant. What mattered was ownership of a fantasy.

Others followed different paths. Stephanie Matto sold sealed fart jars, later switching to fart-jar NFTs after the physical version caused health problems. Farrah Abraham pushed the idea further by offering poop jars and custom scat videos.

Fragmenting the Human Body

Some creators sold nourishment instead of novelty. Alice Lovegood sold bottled breast milk, filmed while pumping, allowing subscribers to watch and then receive the product. Others focused on bodily waste. Creator Kactus Kutie sold urine jars, allowing buyers to request specific diets to alter smell or taste. Multiple sellers listed used menstrual products, vacuum-sealed and priced by "flow strength," often with video proof.

Beyond fluids, the body itself was fragmented.

Some sellers offered hair, beard, and body-hair clippings, sold by weight. Others specialized in performance-based oddities such as slow-motion sneeze or cough videos, mailing used tissues afterward. Buyers selected triggers such as pollen or pepper.

Creator LucyIsLoud sold mute fetish packages—silent videos paired with handwritten notes held against her body during filming. Another creator, “Peekaboo Pumpkin,” a bearded woman, charged for beard-stroking sessions, mailing trimmed whiskers as add-ons.

Pushing the Edge of the Market

Some offerings went further still. After filming high-calorie food challenges, a few creators sold sealed buckets of regurgitated food to emetophile fans.

Regurgitated food refers to swallowed food or liquid returning to the mouth from the stomach or esophagus without nausea, retching, or forceful stomach contractions, often tasting similar to how it did before swallowing.

Others sold mystery body-fluid boxes, containing items such as spit, bath water, foot sweat, or nail clippings.

When shipping liquids became risky, sellers adapted. Digital “scent NFTs” appeared—tokens claiming to encode the smell of worn panties or sweaty socks, often paired with a physical item mailed separately.

Beyond OnlyFans

This trade was not limited to subscription platforms. On eBay, Mercari, and Etsy, sellers listed "used personal items" under coded language. On Reddit, Twitter, and fetish-specific sites such as ScentedPansy, PantyDeal, KinkCoins, ManyVids, and IndieBill, transactions took place openly.

Items sold included used bath water, positive pregnancy test sticks sealed wet with video proof, spit and saliva kits, scent-infused pantyhose, armpit hair and pheromone wipes, toenail clippings and foot-skin shavings, sneeze-soaked tissues, breast-milk jewelry kits, and monthly mystery-fluid subscription boxes.

Prices ranged from a few dollars to several hundred. Payments were handled through CashApp, Venmo, or adult-friendly processors. In most regions, these sales remained legal as long as no sexual services or regulated medical waste crossed state lines.

Why This Market Thrives

These products exist because they fill a space traditional adult content cannot. They are personal, scarce, and symbolic. For buyers, they offer intimacy without interaction. For sellers, they are high-margin extensions layered onto existing content.

What appears absurd on the surface is, in fact, carefully structured. Each item answers a specific demand. Each transforms something ordinary—or taboo—into a controlled commodity.

The Business of Intimacy

This is never a simple exchange of money for images. What creators truly sell is an experience—attention, intimacy, personalization, the feeling of being chosen.

For buyers, it fills emotional gaps, even if briefly. For sellers, it is a calculated service that turns longing into independence. Physical products deepen the illusion, offering proof of a relationship that exists largely in the imagination.

Many top earners use their income to buy property, start new businesses, and fund personal projects. Some invest in cosmetic procedures, describing them not as vanity, but as investments in their brand and confidence.

Cost, Choice, and Control

Critics warn of the cost—the pressure to stand out, the emotional labor, and the gradual push toward extremes. These concerns are real. Yet many creators weigh them against the rewards and make their choice.

As creator Annie Knight once said,

"I don't think you could ever say no to making this amount of money. I love my job. I wouldn't want to do anything else."

Who Holds the Power

OnlyFans did not invent lust. It organized it. It transformed an ancient human impulse into a measurable, trackable economy. Men fuel the system through consumption. Women shape it, control it, and profit from it.

This is not simply a story about adult content. It is about the careful sale of fantasy, attention, intimacy, and even discomfort. It is about turning desire into income.

In the economy of lust, women are no longer just participants.
They are the architects.

And increasingly, the ones who walk away with the power.

Chapter 5

A Village Could Not Stop Dancing

"What we know is a drop; what we do not know is an ocean." — Sir Isaac Newton

When the Body Forgot How to Be Still

Some moments in history feel impossible when read from a safe distance. They sound like myths shaped by fear or imagination. Yet they are recorded plainly, without poetry or exaggeration. The Dancing Plague of 1518 is one such moment, a reminder that the human body can become a stage for forces the mind does not fully understand.

It began in July 1518, in the city of Strasbourg, then part of the Holy Roman Empire. The city was weary. Hunger was common. Disease had passed through more than once. Life pressed hard on ordinary people, and hope was fragile.

On one unremarkable day, a woman named Frau Troffea stepped into the street with her child and a companion. Nothing marked the moment as unusual. There was no music, no celebration, no reason to pause. And then, without warning, her daughter began to move.

She started to dance.

There was no joy in it. No rhythm to follow. Her feet moved as if commanded by something beyond her will. Soon, Frau Troffea herself was dancing too, her face tight with confusion and fear. They tried to stop. They could not.

From Curiosity to Terror

At first, passersby laughed. A strange scene was still a scene, and people are quick to smile at what they do not yet fear. But as the hours passed, the laughter faded. The women did not slow. Sweat soaked their clothes. Their breathing grew sharp and uneven. By nightfall, their feet were cracked and bleeding, yet still they moved.

Others began to join them.

Some stepped forward out of curiosity. Others seemed drawn in, as if pulled by an invisible current. Within days, dozens were dancing. Soon there were hundreds. Men and women, young and old, pregnant women and children, all moving without rest. They danced in streets and homes, in markets and churchyards, collapsing only to rise again when strength returned.

The city watched in horror.

People begged the dancers to stop. Some screamed at their own limbs, pleading with their bodies for mercy. A few collapsed and never stood again. Death came quietly, through exhaustion and failing hearts.

Helpless Authority

Doctors were summoned, but medicine had few answers. They declared that the dancers' blood was overheated and ordered them to dance more, believing movement would restore balance. Musicians were hired. Platforms were built. The madness deepened.

Priests prayed. Officials intervened. Nothing worked.

For weeks, Strasbourg lived inside a nightmare. At its height, nearly four hundred people were caught in the movement. Frau Troffea herself danced for days without rest, until her body finally gave in and carried her to silence.

Searching for Meaning Across Centuries

Long after the streets fell quiet, scholars returned to the event with modern eyes. Some suggested ergot poisoning, caused by mold growing on rye, which produces chemicals capable of disturbing the mind and body. Others pointed to chorea, a neurological disorder whose jerking movements resemble uncontrolled dance, a condition known even in earlier centuries.

Yet no single explanation satisfies every detail.

Strasbourg in 1518 was a city under strain. Crops had failed. Disease had visited repeatedly. Poverty pressed from all sides. When stress becomes unbearable, the human mind sometimes releases it through the body. Fear can spread not only through touch or breath, but through sight, belief, and shared despair.

The Dancing Plague was not merely an illness. It was a collective breaking point.

The Quiet Lesson

This story survives not because it is strange, but because it is human. It tells us that suffering does not always announce itself as pain. Sometimes it arrives as motion. Sometimes the body speaks when the mind has no words left.

And so the dancers of Strasbourg leave behind a truth that still matters: not all plagues travel through the air. Some move through fear, hunger, and hopelessness, passing silently from one exhausted soul to another, until an entire village forgets how to stand still.

Chapter 6

No Peace Without Blood

"Pain insists upon being attended to." — C. S. Lewis

When Calm Arrives Through a Wound

Pain does not always scream. Sometimes it whispers, and when it does, it can be far more unsettling. One such whisper belonged to a young student named Ishan.

Ishan was in Class 12 when he came to see me. Both his hands were wrapped in bandages. He sat very still, his eyes fixed on the floor, as if movement itself might disturb something fragile inside him. For several minutes, he said nothing. The silence was heavy, not empty. It felt like words were pressing against a locked door.

Then he looked up and spoke with sudden honesty.

"I cannot lie, doctor. I will tell you what I am. I will tell you what I see."

I answered calmly and asked what had brought him there. He paused, swallowed, and said quietly, "Please keep me safe." Then he began his story.

The First Cut

Three years earlier, Ishan had fallen from his bicycle. It was an ordinary accident, the kind most children forget within days. His injuries were small. Nothing serious. But as he watched blood run from his hand, something unexpected happened.

He did not feel fear.
He did not feel excitement.

He felt peace.

A deep, steady calm settled over him, unlike anything he had known before. His thoughts slowed. The noise inside him went silent. The world felt manageable again.

Days passed, but the memory of that calm did not fade. Instead, it returned again and again, uninvited. One afternoon, driven by curiosity and longing, he made a small cut on his hand. When the blood appeared, the peace returned instantly.

That was the moment the pattern began.

Chasing Calm, Not Death

Ishan was careful. He did not want to die. He did not want to seriously harm himself. He wanted to live, to study, to grow. What he wanted was that quiet relief, that brief moment when his mind finally rested.

Even the smallest injury became enough. A pinprick. A shallow cut. The sight of blood was all it took for the storm inside him to soften.

He was not drawn to pain. He was drawn to stillness.

Understanding Hemomania

Clinically, experiences like Ishan's are described under a recently proposed term: hemomania. It refers to an excessive and compulsive attraction to blood, especially one's own, not for pleasure or danger, but for emotional regulation.

Hemomania is not yet recognized as a separate psychiatric disorder. It is currently understood as a form of impulse-control behavior, where a person feels an overwhelming urge to see, touch, or sometimes taste their own blood in order to calm intense internal distress.

These individuals are not seeking death. They are seeking reassurance.

As one striking line explains it clearly: they do not want to die; they want proof, in red, that they are still alive.

When the Body Becomes the Language

From a clinical perspective, Ishan's story reminds us of a crucial truth: not all self-injury comes from a wish to end life. For some, blood becomes a signal, a visible anchor that tells the mind it is still in control. It quiets chaos. It slows racing thoughts. It brings grounding.

The relief is temporary, but powerful.

In such cases, the act is not a cry for attention. It is the body speaking when the mind has lost safer words. The wound does not aim to destroy the body, but to silence the noise within it.

Toward Healing, Not Punishment

Understanding this changes how we respond. Fear, shame, or punishment only deepen the struggle. Treatment must focus on helping the person find healthier ways to reach calm, to feel real, present, and safe without harm.

Ishan did not come seeking permission to bleed. He came seeking protection—from himself, and from a pattern he did not fully understand.

His story is a reminder that suffering wears many faces. Some of them are quiet. Some of them bleed. And some of them are simply asking, in the only language they know, for peace.

Chapter 7

The Blood-Thirsty Girl

"The mind is its own place, and in itself can make a heaven of hell, a hell of heaven." — John Milton

A Case That Refused to Be Forgotten

This story comes not from rumor or imagination, but from the life of a senior professor working at a world-renowned medical research institute. He did not encounter this case in textbooks or journals. He encountered it in real time, in a hospital corridor, under harsh white lights.

One afternoon, he was urgently summoned to the emergency ward. On a narrow hospital bed lay a young woman of about twenty-four. She was a research scholar at the university. Her name was Safiya.

She was striking to look at. Blue eyes, sharply defined features, a quiet beauty that drew attention without effort. Her father was Iranian, her mother Irish. Yet the professor sensed, almost immediately, that beneath this calm surface was something profoundly wrong.

The First Encounter with Blood

As he reviewed her medical history, a disturbing pattern emerged.

During her early college years, Safiya had once suffered a minor injury to her hand. The cut was close to the radial artery, and blood flowed freely. For most people, such a sight brings fear or revulsion. Some faint. Some panic.

Safiya felt neither.

Instead, she felt an overwhelming surge of energy, as though something powerful had awakened inside her. What followed stunned everyone. She undressed and began to drink her own blood. Not briefly, not impulsively, but for a prolonged period. She lost a dangerous amount of blood and collapsed unconscious.

Her parents believed it was a suicide attempt. It was not.

A Compulsion That Returned

The behavior did not end with that incident. It returned, again and again. New wounds appeared on her body. Hospital admissions became frequent. Doctors grew alarmed. Eventually, the situation escalated to the point where law enforcement was involved.

During questioning, a small blade was found on her. Further investigation revealed something even more troubling. Safiya had been collecting her blood in containers and drinking it.

This was not ritual. It was not symbolism. It was compulsion.

Understanding Autovampirism

The condition she was suffering from is known as autovampirism, an extremely rare psychiatric phenomenon. Medical literature documents only a handful of such cases worldwide.

One such documented case involved a thirty-five-year-old woman working in a hospital. She stole syringes, injected blood into her own vein, withdrew it, and drank it. Over time, her behavior escalated. She moved from her own blood to animal blood, and eventually to the blood of other people. She became convinced that without blood, she would die.

As the condition progressed, she began hearing voices commanding her to drink blood. She lost sleep. Her thoughts became disorganized. This state was clearly psychotic. She was eventually admitted to a psychiatric institution.

Medical tests, including MRI scans, showed no structural damage to the brain. The illness lived not in damaged tissue, but in distorted belief.

This case, along with only two others, forms the core of what psychiatry recognizes as clinical vampirism, sometimes referred to as Renfield's syndrome.

When Identity Begins to Fade

In such states, the urge to drink blood becomes overpowering. It is not driven by pleasure, cruelty, or fantasy, but by a desperate attempt to feel whole. Patients often describe a belief that their body is empty, broken, or hollow, and that blood is the only substance capable of repairing it.

As the compulsion grows, the sense of self weakens. Identity begins to dissolve. Reality bends.

These conditions are most often linked to severe mental illnesses such as schizophrenia, other psychotic disorders, post-traumatic stress disorder, borderline personality disorder, or antisocial personality traits. Fewer than a hundred cases have been recorded worldwide.

They are rare not because they are imagined, but because they require an extreme convergence of psychological pain and vulnerability.

Safiya's Return to the World

Safiya was treated with antipsychotic medication and intensive psychotherapy. Progress was slow. The urges did not vanish overnight. But gradually, under careful monitoring and structured support, the compulsion weakened.

Day by day, she learned safer ways to ground herself. To feel present. To exist without blood.

Her recovery was not dramatic. It was quiet, fragile, and deeply human.

The Truth Beneath the Fear

Stories like this are often reduced to shock or sensationalism. But stripped of fear, what remains is not a monster.

It is a mind under siege.

Autovampirism is not a hunger for darkness. It is an attempt at relief. A distorted survival strategy formed when the psyche can no longer regulate pain in ordinary ways.

Behind every such case stands not evil, but suffering. Not a creature of legend, but a human being fighting to remain intact.

And that is the truth medicine must never forget.

Chapter 8

The Poison for French Revolution

"Man is not disturbed by things, but by the view he takes of them." — Epictetus

A Summer Without Mercy

France, 1789. Summer arrived, but it brought no relief. The heat pressed down on the land, heavy and unmoving, and the countryside fell into an uneasy silence. Fields stood bare or sickly, birds vanished from the hedges, and the earth itself seemed exhausted.

People worked from dawn to dusk and still returned home hungry. Harvests had failed again and again, and rye, the poor man's grain, grew black and bitter. What little food remained was spoiled, foul-smelling, and dangerous, yet people ate it because hunger allows no pride and no caution.

Weeks passed and then months. Hunger became a constant presence, bending backs and thinning bodies, and slowly something else crept in, invisible but far more dangerous than starvation alone.

When Hunger Learned to Speak

It began as whispers, quiet words shared in doorways and fields. "The nobles are doing this," people said. "They want us to starve." Others claimed that granaries were being burned on purpose, that soldiers were paid to kill livestock, and that villages were being marked for slow death.

No one knew who spoke first, and perhaps no one ever did, because fear has a way of inventing its own voice.

Stories moved faster than facts. From village to village, the same warnings were repeated with growing certainty. People swore they saw armed men near their farms, some heard horses at night, and shadows outside homes took on human shape. Every sound became a signal, and every stranger became a threat.

Fear spread faster than hunger ever could.

The Birth of the Great Fear

As fear tightened its grip, people gathered together for safety. Small groups became crowds, crowds turned restless, panic hardened into anger, and anger demanded release.

Violence followed.

Large houses were attacked first. Manor doors were smashed, records burned, and estates set on fire. Nobles were hunted, beaten, and sometimes killed, and anyone believed to serve them became a target. These were not planned rebellions but desperate acts driven by the belief that survival itself was under attack.

Later, historians would give this wave of panic a name: The Great Fear. It swept through rural France between July 17 and August 3, 1789, leaving terror, ashes, and blood in its wake.

Yet one question refused to fade. How did fear spread so quickly and so completely, without leaders or organization?

The Bread That Betrayed a Nation

Modern historians and physicians began to look beyond politics and rumor, and they looked instead at what people were eating.

For years before 1789, France had suffered from cold, damp weather and long periods without sunlight. Rye crops, especially vulnerable in such conditions, were infected by a toxic fungus that produced powerful chemicals capable of altering the human mind.

Its name is ergot.

Ergot releases substances that interfere with the brain's serotonin system, which controls mood, perception, and emotional balance. In high doses, it can cause hallucinations, paranoia, muscle spasms, and intense fear. One of its compounds, ergotamine, is chemically close to modern hallucinogens.

The poison entered the bread, and the people ate it, because they had no choice.

A Mind Under Siege

Imagine the state of the body and mind then. You are starving, exhausted, already living under inequality and injustice, and now you eat bread that slowly poisons your thoughts.

Your heart races, your senses sharpen too much, you feel watched, you feel hunted, and every rumor sounds true while every shadow confirms your fear.

This mental state is known today as a delusion of persecution, the belief that one is being targeted or attacked without real evidence. It is seen in severe psychiatric conditions, but it can also emerge when fear, stress, hunger, and neurochemical imbalance collide.

In 1789, this collision may have happened on a national scale, as poisoned grain, starving bodies, and frightened minds together formed the quiet chemistry that pushed suspicion into certainty and anxiety into violence.

Revolution Prepared by More Than Politics

The French Revolution had real causes. Crushing inequality, abuse of power, and economic injustice cannot be denied. But beneath those forces, something quieter may also have been at work, softening reason and sharpening terror.

Ergotism is known to cause hallucinations, panic, violence, and even heart failure, and some historians believe it did not create the Revolution but helped prepare the ground by turning fear into conviction and rumor into rage.

The poison did not start the fire, but it may have fed it.

The Quiet Power of Small Things

History often speaks of kings, speeches, and battles, but sometimes the course of nations is bent by something far smaller, such as a mold on grain, a chemical in bread, and a fear that felt real enough to kill for.

The Great Fear reminds us that revolutions are not shaped by ideas alone. They are shaped by bodies, by hunger, and by minds pushed beyond their limits, and sometimes the most powerful force in history is not a sword or a speech, but a silent poison eaten day after day until an entire people can no longer tell fear from truth.

Chapter 9

When Birds Defeated an Army

"History sometimes smiles softly and reminds us that strength does not always wear boots."

When people hear the phrase *Emu War* today, they often laugh. It sounds like a joke, the sort of story shared lightly, as if it belongs to folklore rather than fact. Yet this was no myth. It truly happened, and it remains one of the most unusual military episodes ever recorded.

The year was 1932. The place was Western Australia.

A Land Already Wounded

The land stretched wide and dry beneath an unforgiving sun, glowing gold like a scorched blanket laid across the earth. These were difficult years. The Great Depression had drained savings, thinned hope, and left farmers clinging to the soil for survival. Every seed planted carried not only promise, but fear.

When the crops finally ripened, corn and wheat standing tall after months of struggle, it felt as if relief had arrived at last. Instead, disaster followed.

The enemy was not another nation, not bandits, not soldiers marching under a flag. It arrived on long legs and swift feet. It came as birds.

The Unlikely Invasion

They were emus—tall, brown-feathered creatures with powerful bodies and long necks, some reaching nearly six feet in height. They could run close to fifty kilometers an hour and move for miles without tiring. Most importantly, they did not come alone.

Nearly twenty thousand emus descended upon the farmland in vast numbers, pouring into fields like a living tide. Fences collapsed under their pressure. Wheat fields that had taken months of labor were destroyed in hours. As the barriers fell, rabbits followed, finishing what the emus had begun.

To the farmers, it felt like an invasion. The birds showed no fear and no hesitation. They moved with a strange purpose, as if guided by instinct sharpened into strategy. Watching their livelihoods vanish, farmers stood helpless, feeling as though an unstoppable force had passed quietly through their land, leaving ruin behind.

When the Army Was Called

Desperation drove the farmers to the government. What followed shocked the nation.

In November 1932, Australian soldiers were deployed against the birds as though facing a serious military threat. Armed with Lewis automatic machine guns and supported by military trucks, they were sent with a clear mission: reduce the emu population, protect the wheat, and save the farmers.

Thousands of bullets were fired.

The emus did not respond as expected.

They did not charge blindly or scatter in panic. Instead, they split into small groups, moved unpredictably, and ran in zigzag patterns across open land and rocky hills. They outran vehicles, slipped through gunfire, and even when wounded, continued to flee with astonishing endurance.

Day after day, the guns roared, but the results were humiliating. Ammunition was consumed, morale declined, and the emus disappeared into the hills, only to return again when the soldiers withdrew.

Human strategy had failed.

A Quiet Defeat

The soldiers grew tired and frustrated. Farmers watched in disbelief. Newspapers seized the story with sharp humor, mocking the campaign and questioning the wisdom of sending an army to fight birds. Public ridicule spread faster than any bullet.

After weeks of failure, the Defense Minister ordered the operation halted. The war was over.

The emus had won.

One soldier later reflected on the experience with a strange mix of humor and respect, saying that the birds behaved as though they had a commander of their own, moving with coordination, discipline, and an uncanny ability to outthink human force.

The Lesson History Leaves Behind

No medals were awarded. No victories were declared. The fields were eventually protected not by weapons, but by fences and bounties. Yet the story endured, not because it was amusing, but because it revealed something quietly profound.

Power does not always submit to force. Intelligence does not always yield to weapons. And nature does not bend easily to human plans.

The Emu War stands as a gentle reminder written into history's margins: some battles are lost not because the enemy is strong, but because the world refuses to behave the way humans expect it to.

Chapter 10

A War Started by a Pig

"History often reminds us that great storms can rise from the smallest sparks."

When we think of war, we imagine grand causes and grave intentions. We think of wounded pride between nations, battles for territory, leaders unwilling to step back, and ideologies that refuse compromise. Wars, we believe, begin with thunderous reasons. It is therefore unsettling to learn that one international conflict nearly erupted over something as ordinary as a pig.

Yet this episode, remembered as the Pig War of 1859, is entirely real.

An Island Caught Between Empires

The story unfolds on San Juan Island, a cold and lonely stretch of land often wrapped in mist, lying between the United States and the British Empire, what we now call Canada. For years, both nations claimed ownership of the island, but the dispute remained distant and unresolved. American settlers and British employees lived side by side, farming the same soil and sharing the same harsh weather, unaware that history was quietly setting a trap.

No one expected trouble. Then came the pig.

The Shot That Echoed Too Loudly

One morning, an American settler named Lyman Cutler discovered a pig rooting through his potato patch. The animal belonged to a British employee of the Hudson's Bay Company. Cutler had lost crops before, patience was thin, and hunger was real. Acting out of frustration rather than malice, he took his gun and shot the pig dead.

To him, it was a simple act of protecting his food.

When the British owner arrived and asked if Cutler had killed his pig, Cutler answered honestly and without apology. He explained that the animal had been eating his potatoes. What should have followed was an ordinary human exchange: compensation, raised voices, perhaps an insult or two, and then an end.

Instead, pride entered the conversation.

The British man argued that Cutler should have fenced his land better. Cutler refused responsibility. Words sharpened. The matter grew teeth.

When Ego Replaced Reason

News spread quickly across the island, carried not by facts but by emotion. British officials threatened arrest. American settlers refused to allow it. Each side felt challenged, not materially, but symbolically. Authority was questioned. Respect was wounded.

Soon, officials arrived. Then soldiers followed.

American troops landed on the island to protect their settler. British warships appeared offshore, their cannons visible and ready. Soldiers watched one another through binoculars, tense and uncertain, knowing that a single gunshot could ignite a war between two great powers.

All of this stood balanced on the memory of a dead pig.

The Moment That Saved History

For a brief and frightening moment, war seemed inevitable. Then something rare occurred. A British admiral, recognizing the absurdity of the situation, spoke plainly. He remarked that it would be foolish for two of the world's strongest nations to shed blood over a single pig.

His words pierced the tension.

American leaders agreed to step back. Both sides decided to let their governments resolve the dispute diplomatically. The soldiers remained, but the anger slowly drained away. Men who had stood ready to kill began to talk, share meals, joke, and drink together. Days passed without violence.

No one fired a shot.

A Conflict That Ended Quietly

Years later, San Juan Island officially became American territory. There was no battle to commemorate, no battlefield soaked in blood, no monument raised in stone.

History remembered the incident not for its violence, but for its restraint.

In the field of social psychology, the Pig War is often cited as a classic example of escalation theory, which explains how small conflicts can spiral when pride, fear, and ego replace calm judgment. The trigger is rarely the object itself, but the meaning people attach to it.

In truth, the conflict was never about a pig, or even about potatoes. It was about identity, authority, and the human refusal to step back once pride is challenged.

The Lesson That Still Waits

This strange episode leaves behind a lesson both simple and unfinished. When even one person chooses calm over anger, humility over ego, and reason over reaction, disaster can be avoided. When no one does, history fills with graves.

The Pig War reminds us that peace often survives not because people are wise, but because someone, at the right moment, chooses not to be foolish.

Chapter 11

Cats Rained from the Sky

"The balance of nature is not a status quo; it is fluid, ever shifting, in a constant state of adjustment."
— Rachel Carson

A Silent Emergency in the Rainforests

This story begins on the island of Borneo, the third largest island on Earth, lying deep within Southeast Asia. Shared by Indonesia, Malaysia, and Brunei, Borneo is a land of dense rainforests, heavy monsoon skies, and villages so remote that news often arrived weeks or months late. Life there moved according to rivers, seasons, and the quiet rules of nature.

In 1950, danger arrived without warning. No armies marched in, and no storms announced it. Instead, people began to fall ill. Fever spread from home to home, followed by chills, weakness, and exhaustion that left bodies helpless. The cause soon became clear: malaria, carried by mosquitoes thriving in the warm, wet forests.

The threat was serious, and the response was immediate.

The Solution That Seemed Perfect

The World Health Organization stepped in with what appeared to be a scientific miracle. The answer was DDT, a chemical widely trusted at the time for killing insects. Helicopters flew low over villages and forests, spraying the powder onto rooftops, trees, walls, and soil. The aim was simple: kill the mosquitoes and stop the disease.

At first, it worked. Mosquito numbers fell sharply, and malaria cases dropped. The intervention was praised as a success, a victory of modern science over nature.

But nature was not finished responding.

The Poison That Stayed Behind

DDT did not behave like ordinary chemicals. It did not disappear. It lingered, clinging to leaves, settling into soil, and seeping into water. It is what scientists now call a persistent pollutant, capable of remaining active for years while moving quietly through the food chain.

Insects absorbed the poison first. Birds and small animals then consumed those insects, storing the toxin inside their bodies. As predators fed on them, the poison grew stronger rather than weaker, a process known as biomagnification. Eggshells thinned, reproduction failed, and entire populations quietly collapsed.

Then something unexpected happened.

When the Cats Disappeared

The village cats began to die.

One by one, they vanished from doorsteps and rooftops, victims of poisoned prey. Their absence was noticed only when another presence took over. Rats and mice multiplied rapidly, spilling into homes, food stores, and sleeping areas. With them came fear of plague and other deadly infections. Families panicked. Some abandoned their homes.

A campaign meant to stop one disease had opened the door to another, more terrifying threat.

An Answer That Sounded Like a Joke

Faced with a growing crisis, scientists searched for a solution. What they decided next sounded unbelievable, even absurd. If the cats were gone, they would have to be returned.

In 1960, a plane flew over Borneo's forests carrying an unusual cargo. From the sky, hundreds of cats were released, each lowered safely by a small parachute. As the parachutes touched the ground, the cats landed unharmed, shook themselves, and wandered off into the villages.

Within weeks, the balance began to shift. The mice population declined. Disease retreated. Life slowly steadied itself. Children laughed again at the sight of cats stretching in the sun, unaware that these animals had arrived as part of one of the strangest rescue missions in history.

What the Sky Taught Us

This episode left behind a lesson that still matters. Many ask why mosquitoes are not simply wiped out forever. The answer lies in Borneo. Mosquitoes, like cats, birds, and insects, are part of a complex system. Remove one element without understanding the whole, and the damage spreads in ways no one can predict.

Modern disease control no longer seeks destruction, but balance. In places like Singapore, mosquitoes still exist, yet malaria does not, because ecosystems are managed rather than broken.

Once, the sky over Borneo rained poison. Years later, it rained cats. And in doing so, the island quietly reminded the world that nature does not forgive carelessness, that every action sends ripples through unseen connections, and that when humans forget how deeply life is woven together, even the sky may be forced to correct them.

Chapter 12

Mountain of Death

"In the mountains, there are only two kinds of people—those who listen, and those who are never heard from again." — Reinhold Messner

The Silent Peak

In the northern Ural region of Russia stands a mountain called Kholat Syakhl. In the local language, its name means *Mountain of Death* or *Silent Peak.* Even the name feels like a warning, as though the land itself is asking visitors to stay away. Some stories are more unsettling than ghost tales. They do not shout or threaten. They move quietly, carried by whispers, leaving behind questions that refuse to rest. One such story unfolded here, in the frozen Siberian wilderness, in February 1959.

A Confident Journey

A young engineering student named Igor Dyatlov led a group of eight experienced climbers into the Northern Ural Mountains. These were not careless adventurers. They were strong, trained, and familiar with harsh conditions. Each had conquered difficult terrain before. They believed that no mountain was beyond human effort, no challenge too great to face with skill and courage. None of them imagined that this journey would be their last.

The Search Begins

When the group failed to return, concern turned into alarm. Soviet rescue teams were sent into the mountains, and a wide search began. What they discovered disturbed even the most hardened rescuers. The climbers' tent lay abandoned in a snowy valley. It had been torn open from the inside. Footprints led away from it, heading toward a nearby forest. Some of those footprints were barefoot. It was clear that the group had fled their shelter in the middle of the night, into deadly cold, without proper clothing.

What the Mountain Revealed

Near a cedar tree, two bodies were found. Their hands were frozen and injured, as if they had been desperately trying to climb or gather branches. The remaining bodies were discovered days later, scattered across the snow. Some wore very little clothing. Others wore none at all. Several had broken ribs. One had a fractured skull. One had lost her eyes. Another had lost his tongue. Yet there were no signs of a struggle, no weapons, and no evidence that anyone else had been there. The snow had erased its own footprints.

The Search for Answers

After the bodies were recovered, forensic experts examined the scene with great care. There were no signs of a fight, no weapons, and no evidence that another group had attacked them. No crime could be proven. What remained was a puzzle so strange that, over the years, scientists, psychologists, meteorologists, and mountaineers all tried to explain what might have happened on that mountain. Several possible causes emerged, each explaining part of the tragedy, but none explaining it fully.

Slab Avalanche

One of the earliest explanations was a sudden and violent storm. In the Ural Mountains, weather can change without warning. A powerful blizzard could have filled the air with snow, reduced visibility to nothing, and created intense fear inside the tent. Another related idea is a *slab avalanche*. Unlike a roaring avalanche, a slab avalanche can occur quietly when a hard layer of snow suddenly slides over a softer layer beneath it. Such a movement could have struck the tent, injured some of the climbers, and convinced the group that a larger avalanche was coming. In panic, they may have cut their way out of the tent and fled into the darkness, believing staying inside meant certain death.

Katabatic Winds

Another theory points to katabatic winds, sudden downhill gusts known to occur in polar and mountainous regions. These winds can reach extreme speeds and create powerful pressure changes. At night, they can produce deep, unnatural sounds—howls, roars, or vibrations that resemble engines or approaching forces. For exhausted climbers, such sounds could have created overwhelming fear and disorientation. The wind alone may have made the tent unsafe, forcing the group to abandon it quickly without proper clothing.

Infrasound Panic

Closely linked to the wind theory is the idea of infrasound. Infrasound consists of sound waves below the range of human hearing. Although they cannot be heard, they can be felt by the body and nervous system. Studies show that infrasound can cause anxiety, dizziness, confusion, and a sudden sense of terror. Winds moving around the shape of the mountain may have generated these low-frequency vibrations, silently affecting the climbers' minds. Under such influence, people may feel an intense urge to escape, even without understanding what they are afraid of.

Paradoxical Undressing

Hypothermia is believed to have played a crucial role in the final moments. When the body loses heat faster than it can produce it, the brain begins to malfunction. Judgment weakens, confusion grows, and rational thinking disappears. In severe cases, a phenomenon known as *paradoxical undressing* can occur, where the brain falsely signals that the body is overheating. Victims may remove their clothes despite freezing temperatures. At minus forty degrees Celsius, exposure can be fatal within minutes.

Hypothermia could explain why some climbers were found partially dressed or barefoot, and why their actions appeared irrational.

Theories and Shadows

Each of these explanations answers some questions, but not all. None fully explains every injury, every decision, or the exact sequence of events. This gap in understanding allowed darker theories to appear—secret weapons, radiation, or hidden experiments—but no solid evidence has ever supported them. What remains is a tragedy shaped by nature, fear, and human vulnerability, wrapped in silence and shadow, where the mountain keeps its final truth to itself.

A Lesson Written in Ice

The Dyatlov Pass incident is more than a mystery. It is a reminder of how small human confidence becomes in the face of nature. Mountains do not negotiate. They do not explain. They simply exist, indifferent to belief, skill, or courage.

Chapter 13

The Chicken Without Head

"Truth does not ask permission to surprise us."
— Mark Twain

A Story That Sounds Impossible

The word *chicken* here means exactly that—a real bird. This is not folklore, rumor, or exaggeration. It is a documented historical event, carefully observed and recorded. The story belongs to a rooster named Mike, and it stands as one of the strangest reminders that reality often exceeds imagination. In psychology and science, we return again and again to a simple idea: truth is often stranger than fiction. Nature, in particular, does not always follow the neat rules we expect. Even with all our knowledge, believing we understand everything remains a dangerous illusion.

An Ordinary Day on a Farm

The year was 1945. The place was a small farm in Fruita, Colorado. A farmer named Lloyd Olson was preparing a chicken for dinner. It was an ordinary task, repeated countless times before. In many cultures, when guests arrived, the fattest rooster was chosen and prepared for the table. There was nothing unusual about the moment. Lloyd raised his axe and made a clean cut.

Under normal circumstances, a headless chicken runs briefly, collapses, and dies. That is how it always happens.

But not this time.

When the Impossible Happened

The rooster stood up. It began to walk around the yard. It even tried to crow, though only a strange gurgling sound came from its throat. Lloyd stood frozen, watching something that made no sense. The bird moved with balance and purpose, as if nothing essential had been taken away. The rooster, later named Mike, continued to behave like a living animal, not a dying one.

Mike attempted to peck and scratch for food, but without eyes, he could not see. He could not eat on his own. Yet his body reacted, adjusted, and survived.

A Medical Accident of Rare Precision

What had occurred was not magic, but an extraordinary accident. When the axe fell, it removed the head but spared a critical structure at the back of the skull: the brain stem. This small part of the brain controls vital functions such as breathing, heart rate, balance, and basic movement. It was just enough to keep Mike alive.

Even more remarkably, the carotid artery sealed itself through clotting, preventing fatal blood loss. Nature, in a moment of unlikely precision, allowed life to continue where death was expected.

Life After the Axe

Days passed, then weeks, and then months. Lloyd and his family cared for Mike patiently. Using a dropper, they fed him milk and water and carefully placed food into his throat. Mike did not weaken. He gained weight. His balance improved. His body adapted to its new condition.

Soon, the story reached the newspapers. A chicken living without a head captured the public imagination. Scientists, doctors, and university professors traveled to see Mike for themselves. They examined him closely and confirmed that the reports were true. People came from far away to witness the living proof that biology does not always obey expectation.

Mike lived for eighteen months without a head.

A Quiet Ending

In the end, it was not science or spectacle that ended Mike's life. A single grain of corn became lodged in his throat, and he died quietly. There was no mystery in his death, only in his life.

What Science Learned

Mike's story is still discussed in biology classrooms today. It helped scientists better understand how the brain works, and how survival does not depend on one single control center. The brain is not an on–off switch. It is a layered system, where different parts serve different purposes.

Remove one part, and life may end. Spare another, and life may continue—against all expectation.

After Lloyd earned money by showing Mike to the public, others tried to repeat the event. Every attempt failed. All the chickens died. Mike remained unique.

A Final Reminder

This story offers a quiet but powerful lesson. Humans like to believe that everything follows clear rules, that every event has a reason we can understand. But the world does not always agree. Absence of explanation is not proof of impossibility. Some things simply happen—without order, without meaning, and without asking us to make sense of them.

And that, perhaps, is what makes truth so endlessly surprising.

Chapter 14

The Spider Induced Dance

"The mind has great influence over the body, and maladies often have their origin there." — Molière

A Summer in Southern Italy

This story takes us to Apulia, in southern Italy, during the summer of 1728. The land was warm and generous. Grapevines bent under the weight of ripe fruit, and the season of harvest brought both work and celebration. Villages were alive with movement, music, and shared labor, as people gathered in the fields to pick grapes and prepare for the months ahead.

One day, a group of young girls entered a vineyard to work. As they moved between the vines, a sudden soft scream cut through the air. One of them, Anna Palazzo, had been bitten by a spider. The villagers believed it was a tarantula, a creature feared not just for its bite, but for what it was thought to do to the soul.

Fear Takes Hold

The reaction was immediate. Anna's face appeared swollen. Her breathing slowed. Her eyes seemed wide with terror. Panic spread quickly through the vineyard and into the village. The local doctor, Dr. Nicola Caputos, was called at once. There were no other physicians nearby, no hospitals, and no alternatives.

Later, in his journal, Dr. Caputos wrote words that still unsettle the reader. Anna, he said, appeared almost dead. She was placed on a donkey and carried to the village square like a corpse. Yet there were no cries of mourning, no tears of grief. Instead, something unexpected began to unfold.

Music Instead of Mourning

People arrived carrying tambourines, mandolins, and flutes. The square filled with sound. A fast, repeating rhythm took over the air. It was a tune that would later be known as the Tarantella. The music grew louder. Faster. People began to dance, first cautiously, then wildly.

As the fourth melody played, something extraordinary happened. Anna, who had been unconscious, felt her legs tremble. The crowd gasped. By evening, she stood up. Soon, she was dancing—spinning, twisting, moving with sharp, sudden gestures that reminded onlookers of a spider itself. Her hair fell loose. Her body moved with fierce energy, as if driven by something beyond her will.

At last, exhausted, she collapsed. Night fell. When calm finally returned, Anna opened her eyes.

She was well. The villagers nodded to one another and said, "The poison has left her."

The Spider and the Belief

For centuries, the spider blamed for such events was known as *Lycosa tarantula*, a wolf spider native to southern Europe. Modern science tells us a simple truth: its venom is not dangerous to humans. At most, its bite causes mild pain and slight swelling, no worse than a bee sting.

So what really happened?

Why did people dance until their bodies gave way? Why did exhaustion, not medicine, mark the end of the illness?

The answer lies not in the spider, but in belief.

When the Mind Leads the Body

At that time, people believed the spider's poison had to be driven out through sweat. Dancing was thought to be the cure. This belief spread through communities and became deeply rooted. When one person fell ill, the entire village responded in the same way, reinforcing the idea again and again.

In truth, this was a form of mass psychogenic illness, sometimes called shared psychosis. Fast, repetitive music has a powerful effect on the brain. Rhythm acts directly on the motor cortex, the region that controls movement. Over time, conscious control weakens, and the body begins to move automatically. Pain lessens. Emotion intensifies. The dancer enters a trance-like state.

What looked like poison leaving the body was, in reality, the mind surrendering to rhythm.

Faith, Permission, and Ritual

At first, the Catholic Church opposed this wild dancing. But it could not stop it. Eventually, the Church chose another path. The ritual was accepted and given a sacred frame. It was called the Blessing of Saint Paul. People were allowed to dance, cry, shout, and even tear their clothes, all within a religious setting.

Every summer, the same pattern returned. The same fear. The same music. The same frantic movement. The ritual became tradition.

The Silence That Followed

Modern neuroscience now shows that repeated fast rhythms can reduce pain, increase dopamine, and weaken self-control. When villagers believed the Tarantella would save them, their bodies responded—not because of venom or miracle, but because belief reshaped perception.

In the early twentieth century, life changed. People worked indoors. Public health improved. Shoes became common. Scientific understanding replaced superstition. Slowly, the belief faded.

The spider did not disappear.

But the dance did.

And when belief left the village, the music fell silent, leaving behind a quiet reminder of how deeply the mind can shape the body—and how powerful an idea can be when shared by many.

Chapter 15

Monster in dreams

"When the body sleeps but the mind wakes, fear finds a doorway." — Carl Jung

Between Sleep and Waking

Charles was twenty-two years old when it happened. One night, just as sleep was pulling him under, he woke with a sudden jolt. His eyes were open and his thoughts were clear, yet his body refused to respond. He tried to move his arms and failed. He tried to turn his head, but nothing happened. A crushing weight pressed against his chest, heavy and unmoving, making it hard to breathe.

In the corner of the room, he noticed a dark figure standing perfectly still. It did not speak or move, but its presence felt unmistakable. Many people describe such figures differently—angels, ghosts, ancestors, spirits—but to Charles, it was simply something watching him. Silent. Close. Terrifying.

Fear Without Escape

He tried to scream, but no sound came out. His heart raced wildly as fear spread through his body. Panic took over, sharp and overwhelming, as though danger was inches away and there was no way to escape. The moment felt endless.

Then, without warning, it stopped. His body loosened. He could move again. The pressure vanished. The dark figure dissolved into nothing. The room returned to normal, leaving behind only shock and confusion.

What Really Happened

What Charles experienced is known as sleep paralysis, often accompanied by hypnagogic or hypnopompic hallucinations. It occurs during the fragile boundary between sleep and wakefulness. In this state, the brain wakes before the body does. The muscles remain temporarily paralyzed, a natural safety system meant to prevent us from acting out our dreams. But when consciousness returns too early, dream imagery can spill into waking awareness.

The experience feels intensely real. People may see figures, hear sounds, or feel pressure on their chest. The fear is powerful because the mind is awake, but the body is defenseless.

Misunderstood Experience

Sleep paralysis is far more common than most people realize. Studies suggest that nearly one in three people will experience it at least once in their lifetime. Yet, without medical understanding, many cultures explain it through belief. Stories emerge of night visitors—demons, spirits, ancestors, or divine beings who arrive in the dark.

Across history and geography, the figures change, but the experience remains the same.

Moment of Confusion

In reality, there is no visitor. There is no external presence. What occurs is a brief error in the brain's timing. Dream and reality overlap for a few moments, and the mind, awake but unprotected, tries to give meaning to the fear. The shadow takes shape because the brain demands a reason.

And when the body finally wakes, the visitor disappears—not because it was driven away, not because it chose to leave, but because it was never truly there.

The door closes. The fear fades. And the night returns to silence.

Chapter 16

The Devil that haunts

"The mind can frighten us most when it shows us what we fear least about ourselves." — Carl Jung

A Quiet Confession

Once, a young man named Joshua came to see me. He was twenty-five years old, a software engineer, and deeply God-fearing. Yet the moment he sat down, I could see the weight he was carrying. His fists were clenched. His jaw was tight, as if he were holding something back. For a while, he sat in silence, restless and afraid. I asked him gently to relax.

After a few moments, he spoke. "Sir, I think I am going mad. Thoughts keep flooding my mind. I cannot control them. There is no limit."

I asked him what kind of thoughts he meant. What followed came out in a rush, as if a dam had broken.

Thoughts That Terrified Him

Joshua spoke of sudden, violent ideas that invaded his mind without warning. Thoughts that he might kill someone. That he might cut off a person's hand. That he might stab the people he loved. While driving, he feared someone might step in front of the car. At railway stations, he imagined pushing someone onto the tracks. At night, he lay awake wondering if he might stab his mother while she slept.

His voice trembled as he asked, “Sir, am I possessed by the devil? Have I completely lost my mind? Is this because of some medicine? Please... I need to be saved.”

I gave him water and asked him to breathe slowly.

Then he continued.

While cooking, he felt an urge to mix filth into the food. When he saw a knife, he feared stabbing himself. In church, he worried he might suddenly scream. In office meetings, he feared shouting something obscene without meaning to. He had told his girlfriend. She told her mother. And her mother said he was becoming antisocial—that the devil had entered him.

Naming the Fear

I looked at Joshua and spoke calmly. “This is not possession. This is not the devil.”

Relief washed across his face.

I explained that what he was experiencing is known in psychology as intrusive thoughts. These are unwanted thoughts that enter the mind suddenly. They are often violent, disturbing, or unacceptable to the person who has them. The more one tries to push them away, the stronger they return. Fear feeds them. Anxiety strengthens them. Soon, the mind becomes trapped in a painful loop.

Why the Mind Does This

To help him understand, I gave a simple example. I asked him to look at the wall and tell me its color. He said it was cream. Then I said, "Now look at it again, and do not imagine a red spot on it."

After a short while, I asked him what he saw.

"Red spots," he said quietly.

I smiled and explained, "That is exactly what is happening. The brain does not understand commands like *don't think*. We do not have full control over our thoughts. When we fear a thought, the mind keeps returning to it."

Intrusive thoughts often trouble people who live disciplined, responsible, and moral lives. They are not signs of evil intent. In fact, the fear and disgust these thoughts create are proof that the person does not want to act on them.

You Are Not Alone

Joshua needed counseling, psychotherapy, and at times, medication. But the most important step in his healing was understanding one simple truth: this condition is common, and it is treatable.

Because of shame, many people are afraid to ask questions like these:

Have you ever looked at a knife and imagined hurting someone?
Have you feared harming your parents, children, or loved ones without wanting to?

Have you had thoughts of shouting during prayer, committing a grave religious sin, having unwanted sexual thoughts, eating filth, being naked in public, suddenly dying, or losing control of your body?

If the answer is yes, you are not alone.

The Psychology Behind It

In psychology, intrusive thoughts are most often linked to Obsessive Compulsive Disorder (OCD). They can also appear in severe anxiety, depression, and post-traumatic stress disorder. Monks, priests, and nuns frequently report such thoughts during prayer, often mistaking them for temptation or moral failure. Even Mother Teresa wrote about her inner struggles and sought guidance from Pope John Paul II.

Intrusive thoughts can also appear in neurological conditions such as dementia and Parkinson's disease. In depression, they can become darker and more painful. Most of the time, these thoughts are harmless—but the fear they

create can be overwhelming. In rare cases, that fear can push a person toward despair or suicide.

The Most Important Truth

The truth that matters most is this: intrusive thoughts can be treated. With therapy, understanding, and proper medical care, they lose their power. They fade. They weaken. Peace returns.

And the most comforting truth of all is simple:

Having a terrible thought does not make you a terrible person.

Chapter 17

The Country that sells Virus

"Fear grows fastest when stories travel faster than truth."
— Yuval Noah Harari

A Line That Became a Belief

I recently began reading novels by the Scottish writer Ken Follett. In one of his books, *Whiteout*, a famous scientist casually tells the media, "Look, in China they release some kind of virus every year. We get rid of it with vaccines." It is just one line in a work of fiction, yet it captures a belief that has quietly spread across the world—the idea that most global diseases are born inside Chinese laboratories.

Many argue that this is not an accident, but a narrative shaped, repeated, and amplified until it begins to feel like truth. To understand how such fear takes form, we must look at how stories move faster than facts.

How Fear Is Announced

One day, just as the world believed the coronavirus pandemic was fading and life was slowly returning to normal, our Prime Minister announced that a new variant had appeared and that the situation was frightening. Almost immediately, news followed with alarming speed.

Headlines claimed the pandemic was returning stronger than ever. China, they said, was facing mass deaths. Bodies were piling up. Streets were empty. Hospitals had no space. Lockdowns were returning like a state of emergency.

This news first appeared in American media. Soon, Indian media repeated it, celebrated it, and amplified it. Panic spread faster than verification. Within days, vaccine companies announced confidently that they already had new vaccines ready.

When Reality Went Live

Then something unexpected happened. Malayali bloggers went live from China. Indian students studying there turned on their cameras. Ordinary people living in Chinese cities shared real-time footage. What they showed did not match the headlines. Streets were crowded. Public transport was busy. People walked freely, without masks. Life looked normal.

Slowly, the fear-filled news faded. The urgency vanished. The loud talk of new vaccines went silent.

Science, Speed, and Suspicion

History shows us that deadly diseases like smallpox were eliminated through vaccines, but that process took decades of research, trials, and careful observation. Science moved slowly, cautiously, and transparently. In contrast, the COVID vaccines arrived within months. Governments across the world enforced rules that made daily life almost impossible without vaccination.

In India, vaccine certificates even carried the Prime Minister's photograph. First, people were told the vaccine would prevent infection. When that claim failed, they were told it would prevent severe illness. When that too weakened, they were told it would prevent death. When even that became uncertain, people joked bitterly that at least they had not promised heaven.

Many began calling the vaccines a failure, claiming that thousands died due to side effects and that many more suffered long-term illness. Governments and vaccine supporters dismissed these concerns as coincidence and demanded proof from ordinary people. Others asked a simple question: if such claims were widespread, should it not be the responsibility of governments and pharmaceutical companies to investigate openly, instead of asking poor citizens to prove complex medical links?

Some warned against scientism—the blind belief that anything developed quickly in the name of science must be correct.

Who Benefited While Millions Suffered

While millions lost jobs, loved ones, and dignity, some industries thrived. E-commerce giants like Amazon, Flipkart, and Walmart expanded rapidly. Video platforms such as Zoom, Microsoft Teams, and Google Meet became necessities. Streaming services turned into daily habits. Food delivery apps flourished. Telemedicine and online education exploded. Home fitness equipment sold at record levels.

Pharmaceutical companies—Pfizer, Moderna, AstraZeneca, Johnson & Johnson—made profits known only to themselves. In a time of global suffering, certain businesses quietly prospered.

Chaos on the Ground

In India, the sudden lockdown of March 2020 was announced with just four hours' notice. Millions of migrant workers were stranded. People walked hundreds of kilometers without food or water. Many slept on railway tracks. Unofficial estimates suggest over a thousand died during that journey alone. There was little coordination between central and state governments. Decisions were taken without understanding local realities.

Then came public rituals—clapping hands, lighting lamps at 6 pm—to chase away the virus. Crores participated. Some even claimed there was science behind it. The Aarogya Setu app was made mandatory, despite many not owning smartphones. Privacy concerns followed. Curfew rules were confusing. Odd-even shop systems created crowding instead of safety. Red, orange, and green zones made little sense on the ground.

Vaccine registration portals failed. Vaccines were unavailable. Private hospitals charged heavily. During the second wave in April–May 2021, hospitals ran out of oxygen, leading to countless deaths. Warnings had existed, but preparation failed. Political rallies and mass gatherings like the Kumbh Mela were allowed, later identified by the World Health Organization as super-spreader events.

Even in late 2022, random testing and quarantine rules returned as cases declined. Some claimed this benefited luxury hotels. Accurate data was often unavailable. Police enforcement was harsh. People were treated like criminals rather than citizens.

The Question History Will Ask

Looking back, many wonder whether future generations will even believe that 21st-century governments responded this way to a disease with a reported mortality rate of around two percent. This chapter is not about proving who is right or wrong. It is about understanding how fear, power, money, and uncertainty combine.

In that mixture, stories grow stronger than facts. Narratives harden into belief. And suspicion becomes easier than patience.

In the end, the most dangerous virus may not be made in a laboratory, but inside the human mind—when fear is allowed to spread without restraint, and truth is left struggling to catch up.

Chapter 18

The Toxic Body

"Nothing in life is to be feared, it is only to be understood." — Marie Curie

The Business of Fear

There are people who understand fear well. They know how to touch it softly, awaken it slowly, and then turn it into profit. Governments often do little to stop them, because fear keeps the public occupied—busy enough to overlook the dangers that truly matter. When fear is carefully directed, it distracts rather than protects.

A Visit That Should Never Have Happened

A few days ago, two women came to see me. One of them was critically unwell. Her sister, an educated and successful professional working for a multinational company in Bangalore, had devoted her life to caring for her. An officer accompanied them. Two weeks earlier, the younger woman had been admitted to the ICU. It was not a suicide attempt. It was something far more disturbing.

They had believed an idea they heard somewhere—that drinking large amounts of water would flush all germs and toxins out of the body. So she drank water. Not a little. According to her sister, nearly twelve liters in a single day.

Even five liters taken at once can be fatal. That amount is considered a lethal dose.

What followed was simple and terrifying. Her sodium and potassium levels collapsed. She lost consciousness. The medical terms are hyponatremia and hypokalemia. This was not the act of a mentally ill person. This danger stands before all of us, hidden behind attractive ideas.

The Myth of the "Toxic Body"

The belief that the human body is filled with toxins has quietly entered many minds. Books titled *Remove Toxins from the Body* or *Complete Detox* sell rapidly. Their covers often show smiling, slim women, suggesting that health, beauty, and confidence lie just one method away. Thousands of Malayalam YouTube videos promise to "clean" the body from within.

This idea is carefully planted. The so-called detox methods are not just misleading; they are scientifically absurd. There is no disagreement about this among medical professionals. Many who promote detoxification do not understand poisoning, physiology, or even basic biology.

They promise cleansing through special diets, certain "natural" foods, excessive water intake, forced sweating, or repeated stomach cleansing. Do this daily, they say, and all toxins will vanish.

What Poison Really Means

A poison is anything that harms the body. Science is clear on one principle: the dose makes the poison. In small amounts, many substances are harmless or even essential. In large amounts, they become dangerous. That is why we have kidneys, a liver, lungs, and skin. These organs remove waste efficiently every second of our lives. Are we truly suggesting they can be replaced by lemon water?

Remember this as well: natural does not mean safe. Sodium is a chemical. Chlorine is a chemical. Together they form salt—useful in moderation, deadly in excess. Snake venom is natural. So are many toxic plants. Every green leafy vegetable contains chemicals, often along with pesticide residues. Quantity and balance matter, not labels.

The human body hosts trillions of microorganisms. Bacteria alone may make up 1–3 percent of our total body weight. In fact, we may carry more bacterial cells than human cells. Life inside us depends on balance, shaped by millions of years of evolution. If toxins truly needed removal, the body already has the tools.

What we need is simple: balanced food, physical activity, clean air, and mental well-being.

Why Detox Feels Good

Detox practices feel good because they reward everyone involved. The writer earns money. The follower feels hope.

The routine gives a sense of control. The placebo effect creates a temporary feeling of cleanliness and achievement. But the cost is real—financial loss, nutritional deficiency, dehydration, and dangerous electrolyte imbalance.

There are no global regulatory bodies overseeing detox practices. No standard scientific guidelines exist. Yet people follow them like faith, driven by personal testimonials. These stories become powerful advertisements. Crores of rupees are spent on marketing, with almost no regulation—especially in India.

The Poisons We Refuse to See

Now let us talk about real toxins. One hundred and eleven of the world's 150 most polluted cities are in India. Cities like Delhi regularly disappear under thick smog. This is one of the greatest public health crises of our time.

Fireworks, a single day of celebration, release sulfur dioxide, nitric oxide, and carbon dioxide into the air. These gases linger for days and can even cause acid rain. Bursting fireworks for one day in a single household is like one person sitting in a closed room while forty people smoke cigarettes around them. Passive smoking is harmful. This is far worse.

And yet, how often do we discuss this?

According to the Air Quality Life Index, air pollution reduces average life expectancy in India by several years. In cities like Delhi, this can rise to nine or ten years. The diseases it causes are many and severe.

Fear as a Distraction

Instead of confronting these realities, people are taught to fear imaginary toxins inside their bodies. Those who profit from fear thrive on distraction. They sell comfort, not truth. And while we worry about invisible poisons that do not exist, the real ones quietly fill the air we breathe.

Fear is easy to sell. Truth requires courage.

Chapter 19

Fear Mongering

"What we feel outside often begins quietly inside the mind." — William James

The Rise of a Popular Fear

Not very long ago, people rarely spoke about *negative energy*. Today, the phrase is everywhere. We hear about houses filled with negative energy, rooms that must be cleansed, objects that attract bad vibrations, and people who supposedly carry harmful energy within them. The words flow easily through conversations, social media, television, and endless online videos.

From people recording advice on mobile phones to famous gurus spending lakhs on promotion, everyone seems to know how to remove negative energy from your life. Mainstream media publishes articles about it regularly. Even respected voices and health experts sometimes use the term. The idea has quietly settled into daily language, almost unquestioned.

But let us pause for a moment and ask a simple question.

What exactly is negative energy?

An idea without a definition

Ask ten people what negative energy means, and you will receive ten different answers. Some say rock salt removes it. Others speak of prayer, mantras, rituals, sacred objects, crystals, lemons, or incense. Each person adds imagination, belief, and tradition to the idea. Superstition and pseudoscience blend effortlessly, creating something that feels meaningful but remains unclear.

So let us slow down and ask the question properly.

What is energy?

What Science Means by Energy

In physics, *energy* has a precise meaning. It refers to measurable quantities such as motion, heat, electricity, or force. Scientists use words like positive and negative in very specific contexts—gravitational fields, electrical charges, quantum states, or temperatures below zero.

Consider a simple example. A battery has a positive and a negative terminal. If you touch the negative terminal, does negative energy flow into your body? If you touch the positive one, does positive energy enter you? Nothing of the sort happens. These terms have meaning only within scientific systems. Outside that context, they are just labels.

The "negative energy" spoken about in popular videos has no connection to scientific energy at all. The word is borrowed, but the meaning is entirely invented.

Why the Myth Survives

If science is clear that this kind of negative energy does not exist, why do we hear so little about that fact? The answer is simple. Explaining misconceptions is not as attractive as selling solutions. Talking about removing negative energy gains views, followers, and income. Saying that it does not exist rarely does.

So if there is no such energy, what are people actually feeling?

The Feeling Is Real

It is true that we sometimes feel uncomfortable around certain people or uneasy in certain places. That experience is real. But its cause is not invisible energy floating in the air.

Human reactions are shaped by many factors—appearance, language, tone, body posture, past experiences, culture, class, religion, and personal memories. The brain constantly reads these signals and decides whether something feels safe or threatening. It often makes mistakes, confusing imagined danger with real danger.

That discomfort, fear, or tension is what many people call negative energy.

Nothing flows from another person into you. There is no transfer of force or vibration. What happens is internal interpretation.

The Power of Interpretation

The same situation can create completely different experiences in different people.

Imagine a man telling an elderly rural woman, "Aunty, you look very beautiful today." She may feel disturbed. In her belief system, such praise could invite the *evil eye*. Anxiety follows. She worries that her health or luck may suffer. The experience feels negative.

Now imagine the same words spoken to a young American woman. She smiles. Her confidence rises. Her mood improves. The experience feels positive.

The words are identical. The speaker is the same. Nothing external changed. Only interpretation did.

Where Energy Truly Lives

What we label as positive or negative energy is created inside the brain. Joy, fear, sadness, excitement, and comfort are produced by neurotransmitters and neural circuits responding to our beliefs and experiences. A color that calms one person may unsettle another. A song that brings peace to one heart may awaken pain in another. A place that feels safe to one may feel threatening to someone else.

The difference is not energy in the air.

It is chemistry in the mind.

The Quiet Truth

When people speak of negative energy, they are often speaking about their own inner world—their fears, memories, conditioning, and expectations. The sensation feels external, but its origin is internal.

The energy was never outside.

It was always within.

Chapter 20

Great Molasses Flood

"The illusion of safety is often strongest just before it collapses." — Sigmund Freud

A Familiar Giant in the City

On a cold January afternoon in 1919, Boston was living an ordinary day. Dock workers unloaded ships along the harbor. Children played near the streets, their laughter mixing with the salty smell of the sea. In the North End stood a massive steel tank—tall, dark, and silent—filled with molasses. It had been there for years. People passed it every day without a second thought. What is familiar often feels safe, and what feels safe is rarely questioned.

That feeling, however, was an illusion.

The tank contained about 8.7 million liters, or 2.3 million gallons, of molasses, nearly three and a half Olympic swimming pools worth of thick syrup. It stood roughly 50 feet tall and 90 feet wide, built hastily during a time of urgency. The molasses was meant for industrial alcohol, used in making ammunition and spirits. World War I had just ended, and Prohibition was approaching. Demand was high. Speed mattered more than caution.

When Certainty Shattered

Without warning, the tank burst.

A roar louder than thunder tore through the neighborhood. Steel walls split open, and a massive wave of molasses surged into the streets with terrifying force. It moved at nearly 35 miles per hour, as fast as a man could run. Narrow streets flooded instantly. Buildings were crushed. Wooden beams snapped like matchsticks. In a single moment, ordinary life collapsed.

People were caught completely unprepared. Some were thrown to the ground. Others were trapped where they stood, sinking into the thick syrup. Horses panicked and struggled until they could no longer move. Carts overturned. Cries for help echoed through the streets. Minds froze. Fear spread faster than reason.

In the winter cold, the molasses thickened rapidly. With every passing minute, it tightened its grip, turning panic into paralysis. Fear was no longer just an emotion. It became physical—heavy, suffocating, and inescapable.

Human Fragility Exposed

The flood revealed a harsh truth. Strong buildings failed. Powerful animals became helpless. Everyday tools were useless. Human confidence in industry, steel, and progress shattered in seconds. The disaster exposed how fragile control truly is when systems built without care suddenly break down. Certainty vanished, leaving only shock.

This was not just an engineering failure. It was a psychological one. The belief that "nothing has happened before, so nothing will happen now" collapsed under the weight of reality.

When Fear Gave Way to Compassion

Yet, in the midst of terror, something else emerged.

People rushed to help without hesitation. Neighbors pulled strangers from the sticky flood with bare hands. Firefighters, police officers, and sailors from nearby ships waded into the molasses, moving slowly, fighting its weight with every step. Social boundaries disappeared. In that moment, there were no strangers—only human beings in danger.

This sudden solidarity revealed a deep instinct. When life is threatened, compassion often rises before fear has time to divide. Crisis stripped away status, class, and distance, leaving only shared vulnerability.

Loss, Trauma, and Memory

Rescue efforts continued for hours. Waiting became unbearable, filled with hope and dread. Some victims could not be reached in time. When the streets were finally cleared, 21 people were dead, and more than 150 were injured. These were not just numbers. Each death carried a name, a family, and a story.

For weeks afterward, the smell of molasses lingered. It clung to streets, walls, and clothing. Even years later, people said the city smelled sweet on hot days. Such sensory reminders kept the trauma alive, pulling the past into the present again and again.

From Grief to Accountability

Grief soon turned into anger. The public demanded answers. A long legal battle followed, lasting nearly six years. Investigations revealed that the tank had been poorly designed, badly constructed, and never properly tested. Warnings had been ignored. Leaks had been painted over instead of repaired.

Trust was broken.

Society needed accountability—not only to assign blame, but to restore a sense of order and safety. The disaster was no longer seen as an unavoidable accident, but as a preventable tragedy born of negligence and haste.

Pain That Forced Change

Out of suffering came reform. Building regulations were strengthened. Large industrial structures were subjected to stricter inspection. Companies were made legally responsible for public safety. The flood reshaped how engineering, corporate responsibility, and public risk were understood.

Pain forced learning. Loss demanded change.

The Deeper Meaning

Today, the Great Molasses Flood is remembered as one of the strangest disasters in American history. But beneath its oddness lies a deeper truth. It is a story of blind trust in familiar dangers, of sudden shock and collective trauma, of human helplessness and human courage.

It reminds us how societies ignore risks until disaster strikes, how people unite when systems fail, and how meaningful lessons are often learned only after irreversible loss.

The Great Molasses Flood is not merely about a tank that burst. It is about fear and carelessness, kindness and responsibility, and a quiet truth we prefer to forget: safety is never automatic. It must be questioned, built carefully, and protected every single day.

Chapter 21

The Day the Sky Broke

"Sometimes the earth remembers what the human mind cannot explain." — Carl Gustav Jung

The Day the Sky Broke

In the summer of 1908, deep inside the vast silence of Siberia, something happened that unsettled both the land and the limits of human understanding. This was a region untouched by cities, machines, or crowds. Ancient forests stood undisturbed, and life moved slowly, following rhythms older than memory.

Then, without warning, the sky itself seemed to tear apart.

On the morning of June 30, 1908, around 7:14 a.m., a massive explosion ripped through the atmosphere above the Podkamennaya Tunguska River. The force was unimaginable. In a single instant, nearly 2,000 square kilometers of forest were flattened. An estimated 80 million trees were knocked down, all lying in the same outward direction, as if swept aside by an invisible hand. The ground shook violently. The air burned. And then, just as suddenly, silence returned.

Destruction Without a Scar

What disturbed people most was not only the scale of destruction, but what was missing.

There was no impact crater.

No deep wound in the earth. No obvious mark pointing to the source of such power. The forest lay broken, but the land itself showed no sign of collision. For the human mind, this absence was deeply unsettling. People find comfort in visible causes. A hole in the ground, a shattered object, something to point at and name. Tunguska offered none of that.

The destruction was undeniable, yet the cause remained invisible.

Voices from the Witnesses

Although the region was sparsely populated, eyewitnesses described a terrifying spectacle. One of the most detailed accounts came from Semyon Semenov, recorded years later by Russian scientist Leonid Kulik. Sitting outside his home near the Vanavara trading post, Semenov saw the sky split open. Fire appeared high above the forest. The heat became unbearable, as if his clothes were burning. A powerful blast threw him several meters through the air. The ground trembled. Windows shattered. Metal locks snapped. The sound, he said, was like falling rocks and firing cannons combined.

People hundreds of kilometers away felt the shockwave. Seismic stations across Eurasia recorded tremors. Atmospheric pressure waves circled the globe.

And still, there was no crater.

Science Arrives Late

It took more than a decade before scientists could study the site. Political upheaval and the region's extreme isolation delayed investigation. In 1921, Leonid Kulik led the first Soviet expedition to the area, convinced a massive meteorite had struck the earth. When his team finally reached the center of the blast zone in 1927, they expected to find a crater.

Instead, they found something stranger.

At the center, trees stood upright but stripped of branches, scorched and lifeless. Farther away, trees lay flattened outward in a vast radial pattern. Later surveys showed the devastated area covered about 2,150 square kilometers, shaped like a gigantic butterfly, with wings stretching nearly 70 kilometers across.

Power without impact. Destruction without collision.

The Invisible Cause

Over the decades, more than 1,000 scientific papers have been written about Tunguska. Energy estimates range from 3 to 30 megatons of TNT, comparable to a large nuclear explosion. Modern science now strongly supports one explanation: a mid-air explosion, or *airburst*, caused by a stony asteroid or icy comet fragment roughly 50–60 meters wide.

As the object entered Earth's atmosphere at extreme speed, atmospheric pressure and heat caused it to disintegrate several kilometers above the ground. The explosion released enormous energy, flattening the forest below, but leaving no crater because the object vaporized before impact. The event closely resembles a smaller modern example—the Chelyabinsk meteor of 2013, which exploded in the air and injured over 1,500 people without striking the ground.

A Psychological Shock

Yet Tunguska is not unsettling only because of physics. It is unsettling because of psychology.

The event challenged a deep human belief: that every disaster leaves behind a clear reason and a visible source. Here, nature displayed overwhelming power without leaving a clear mark. Without an object to blame, imagination rushed in. Mystery filled the space where certainty should have been.

The explosion reminded humanity how fragile control truly is. How safety can vanish without warning. How knowledge, no matter how advanced, can still fall silent before nature.

A Quiet Lesson

The Tunguska forest became a silent classroom. It taught that enormous forces can pass through the world without leaving obvious scars. That danger does not always announce itself. That absence can be more frightening than presence.

Today, Tunguska remains the largest impact-related event in recorded human history. But its deeper significance lies not only in what happened, but in what did not. No crater. No debris. No final certainty.

Only questions.

And perhaps that is its greatest lesson. Some events are not meant to be neatly understood. Some mysteries leave their deepest mark not on the land, but on the human mind, reminding us—quietly and firmly—of humility.

Chapter 22

The Alien Attack

"Some mysteries are quiet. They do not shout. They simply wait." — Agatha Christie

A Ship Without Voices

In December 1872, a strange discovery was made in the open Atlantic Ocean. A merchant ship named The Mary Celeste was found drifting calmly near the Azores. Her sails were partly raised. Her course was steady. She looked ready to continue her journey.

But there was no one on board.

The captain, his wife, their young daughter, and the entire crew had vanished. The sea around the ship was silent. No distress signals. No signs of panic. Only absence.

What Was Not Missing

What disturbed people most was not damage, but order. The cargo was intact. The ship carried 1,701 barrels of denatured alcohol, and though a few were empty, most were untouched. Personal belongings were still in place. The captain's instruments lay neatly arranged. Food and water supplies were sufficient. There were no broken rails, no bloodstains, no evidence of struggle or piracy.

The ship had not been wrecked by a storm. It had not been attacked. It had not been looted.

And yet, the lifeboat was gone.

Why Silence Frightens the Mind

Psychologically, this kind of mystery is deeply unsettling. When there is destruction, the mind finds meaning. When there is chaos, fear has a shape. But the Mary Celeste offered neither. It presented calm without life, order without people.

Humans expect danger to leave marks behind. A scream. A wound. A broken thing. Here, there was nothing. The silence itself became the threat. It forced people to face a disturbing idea—that disaster can arrive quietly, without warning or trace.

The ship became a mirror for human anxiety. If people could disappear while everything else remained unchanged, what did that say about safety? About control? About certainty?

What Investigators Found

When the ship was examined, a few details stood out. There was about 3.5 feet of water in the hold, not enough to sink the ship, but enough to cause concern. One of the pumps had been dismantled, suggesting it was not working properly. The alcohol cargo included barrels made of red oak, known to leak vapors more easily than standard barrels.

Nothing proved disaster. But nothing felt fully safe either.

The Most Likely Explanation

Today, historians and maritime experts do not believe in pirates, monsters, or ghosts. The strongest explanation is a combination of ordinary problems that together led to an extraordinary outcome.

Leaking alcohol barrels likely released fumes. Though invisible, such fumes could create fear of explosion. At the same time, a clogged or dismantled pump may have convinced ** Captain Benjamin Briggs that the ship was taking on water and could sink. Rough seas or a waterspout may have worsened his anxiety.

Fearing an explosion or sudden sinking, Briggs may have ordered everyone into the lifeboat, intending to stay close to the ship until danger passed. A rope likely tied the lifeboat to the Mary Celeste. But wind, waves, or a snapped line may have separated them. The small boat, overloaded and vulnerable, would not have survived long.

The ship sailed on.

The people did not.

Why the Mystery Endures

There is no single, final answer because no one lived to tell what happened after the crew left the ship. No bodies were found. No lifeboat was recovered. The sea kept its secret.

Fiction later magnified the mystery. Writers like Arthur Conan Doyle added supernatural elements that captured public imagination. But the real story is quieter—and perhaps more frightening.

A Lesson in Uncertainty

The Mary Celeste is remembered not for what was found, but for what was missing. A ship ready to sail. A cargo untouched. A world intact. And yet, no human presence.

It reminds us that not all dangers announce themselves. Some arrive without noise. Some leave no scars. And some mysteries do not seek to be solved.

They simply remain—
floating quietly,
waiting in silence,
long after the storm has passed.

Chapter 23

Meat Rain

"The most frightening moments are not those of danger, but those in which the world stops making sense."
— Hannah Arendt

An Ordinary Sky

In the spring of 1876, life moved quietly in a rural part of Kentucky, near a small farming community. The fields were open, the air was still, and the day carried no sign of disturbance. The sky was clear and familiar, the kind people trusted without thought. Nothing warned those below that the ordinary order of things was about to break.

Then, without sound or signal, raw meat began to fall from the sky.

When the Impossible Arrived

Chunks of flesh dropped suddenly, striking the ground in scattered pieces. They did not drift like leaves or dissolve like rain. They fell heavy and real, landing in fields and yards where moments earlier there had been nothing. People froze, looking upward in shock, searching the empty sky for an explanation that never came.

There was no storm. No lightning. No explosion. The silence made it worse. Fear did not rise from immediate danger, but from confusion. The sky, which had always behaved in predictable ways, had done something impossible.

The Shock to the Mind

Psychologically, events like this strike deeper than disasters with clear causes. When a storm destroys a house, the mind can understand it. When fire burns, fear has a shape. But when raw meat falls from a clear sky, the mind has nowhere to place the experience.

The fear was not of the meat itself. It was of what the event suggested. If the sky could behave like this once, what else could happen without warning? The sense of safety that rests quietly beneath daily life cracked in an instant.

For those who witnessed it, the memory lingered. The image returned in quiet moments, not as terror, but as unease. It reminded them that certainty is fragile, and order is not guaranteed.

The Searching for Meanings

Naturally, people searched for explanations. Some believed it was a divine sign. Others whispered of curses or omens. A few even tasted the meat, trying to understand what had fallen from above. Samples were examined, and the strange rain slowly moved from fear into curiosity.

Scientists later confirmed that the material was real animal tissue—muscle and lung, not plants or bacteria. This ruled out early ideas such as *Nostoc*, a jelly-like cyanobacterium once suggested as an explanation.

The Most Accepted Explanation

The most widely accepted explanation came from Dr. L. D. Kastenbine, a local physician. He proposed that a flock of turkey vultures or black vultures had been flying overhead. Vultures feed on carrion, often consuming large amounts of decaying flesh. When startled or threatened, they have a well-known defense mechanism: they regurgitate their stomach contents to lighten their weight and escape quickly.

If a large flock was startled at the same moment, the result could have been a sudden, coordinated release of half-digested meat, scattered over a small area below. The smell, texture, and type of tissue found matched what vultures commonly eat. This explanation, supported by later analysis and referenced by *Scientific American*, remains the most plausible scientific answer.

Why the Unease Remains

Even with a logical explanation, the Kentucky Meat Shower continues to unsettle. Not because it was dangerous, but because it broke an unspoken rule. The sky is not supposed to behave that way. And when it does, even briefly, the human mind struggles to regain balance.

The event caused no deaths, no lasting damage. Yet it lives on in history because it challenged certainty. It reminded people that nature does not always announce itself, and that the most unsettling events often arrive quietly, without warning, and without drama.

A Quiet Reminder

The Kentucky Meat Shower of 1876 remains one of the strangest recorded events in American history. It is remembered not for destruction, but for confusion. Not for loss, but for the moment when the world stopped behaving as expected.

Even today, the story carries a soft unease. It reminds us that the rules we trust are habits, not guarantees. And sometimes, without thunder or fire, the sky reminds us how little control we truly have.

Chapter 24

Beer Flood

"Sometimes, even the most familiar things can turn strange in a single moment."
— Edmund Burke

An Ordinary City, An Unthinkable Event

In October 1814, London was moving through another ordinary day. Taverns were busy, streets were narrow and loud, and beer flowed as it always had. Porter was not a luxury; it was a daily companion, safer to drink than water and woven deeply into working-class life. No one imagined that this familiar drink would suddenly become the face of disaster.

Yet that is exactly what happened.

When the Barrels Gave Way

Inside the Horse Shoe Brewery on Tottenham Court Road stood enormous wooden vats used to ferment porter. One of them was immense—about 22 feet tall, built to hold vast quantities of beer. Inside, fermentation was ongoing, quietly building pressure. Iron hoops held the wooden staves together, and such hoops were known to loosen from time to time. It was considered routine. No alarm was raised.

Then one iron band slipped.

The vat ruptured with explosive force. The pressure did not release gently. It tore the structure apart and triggered a chain reaction, bursting nearby vats as well. In seconds, more than 320,000 gallons (around 1.47 million liters) of beer surged out of the brewery.

A Flood No One Could Understand

A massive wave of beer rushed into the surrounding neighborhood of St. Giles, one of the poorest areas of London. Buildings collapsed under the sudden weight. Walls gave way. Streets turned into rivers. People were knocked down, trapped, and drowned.

Eight people lost their lives, most of them women and children, crushed or suffocated inside their homes. This was not a place built to withstand force. It was crowded, fragile, and already struggling.

What made the scene so disturbing was not only the destruction, but the nature of it. Beer—something warm, social, and familiar—had become deadly. The mind struggled to accept what the eyes were seeing.

When the Familiar Turns Threatening

Psychologically, disasters like this cut deeper than fires or storms. Fire looks dangerous. Storms sound violent. But beer belongs in mugs and barrels, in laughter and routine.

When something ordinary becomes lethal, confusion comes before fear.

People hesitate. They question reality. For a moment, nothing feels stable.

This is how a quiet sense of safety breaks—not through terror alone, but through disbelief.

Judgment Without Blame

A court later ruled the disaster an "Act of God." The brewery was not held criminally responsible. At the time, pressure buildup in wooden vats was considered a known risk of brewing, not negligence. Still, the event left a deep mark on public consciousness.

The absence of punishment did not mean the absence of learning.

Change Born from Shock

After the flood, breweries across Britain reconsidered their practices. Large wooden vats were gradually replaced with concrete and reinforced containers, reducing the risk of catastrophic failure. Safety standards improved—not because of foresight, but because of tragedy.

Loss forced reform.

Why the Story Endures

The London Beer Flood is remembered not just for its oddity, but for its meaning. It showed how fragile control can be. How systems we trust quietly can fail without warning. How danger does not always arrive dressed as danger.

The event did not roar like a war or burn like a firestorm. It arrived through something people knew well and welcomed daily. That is why it stayed in memory.

A Quiet Lesson

Long after the beer dried and the streets were rebuilt, the story remained. Not as a tale about alcohol, but as a reminder. That the ordinary can turn strange in an instant. That safety is not guaranteed by familiarity. And that when the world shifts suddenly, the human mind is left to search for meaning amid surprise, fear, and disbelief.

The London Beer Flood did not just soak a city.
It unsettled the trust people placed in the everyday.

Chapter 25

Sound of Devil

"Some sounds are not heard with the ears alone. They are felt." — R. Murray Schafer

A Sound That Would Not Leave

Beginning in the 1940s, in the small town of Taos, New Mexico, something unusual entered daily life. It did not arrive suddenly. It did not announce itself. Instead, it settled quietly into the background, a low and steady hum that some residents began to notice and could never fully escape.

It was not loud. It did not interrupt conversation or drown out other sounds. Yet for those who heard it, once noticed, it became impossible to ignore. The hum followed them into quiet rooms and open spaces, into the stillness of night and the calm of early morning. It was always there, steady and persistent.

And yet, many people heard nothing at all.

When Experience Divides People

This difference made the hum deeply unsettling. Those who heard it struggled to describe it. Some called it a low drone, others a vibration, a distant engine, or a faint buzzing felt more in the chest than in the ears. Those who could not hear it often struggled to believe it existed at all.

The sound did not behave like ordinary noise. It did not come from a clear direction. It could not be recorded reliably. It did not stop when people moved away. This created a quiet divide—between those who lived with the hum and those who did not.

To be heard by only a few is to invite doubt. And doubt, when repeated, slowly becomes isolation.

The Weight of Uncertainty

What troubled residents most was not the sound itself, but the absence of explanation. There was no visible source. No machine to point to. No single cause that could be named and fixed. Without answers, the mind returned to the hum again and again, searching for meaning.

Psychologically, this kind of mystery is exhausting. A noise that does not end, does not explain itself, and does not belong to anything visible slowly wears down patience and trust. Frustration builds. Anxiety follows. Some people reported difficulty sleeping, concentrating, or relaxing. Others felt a growing sense of loneliness, especially when doctors, neighbors, or officials told them nothing was there.

The hum became more than a sound. It became a question without rest.

Science Looks for a Cause

Over the decades, scientists, engineers, and researchers attempted to understand the phenomenon. Studies were conducted, including investigations by Los Alamos National Laboratory, yet no single source was identified. Measurements often failed to detect anything unusual, even when residents insisted the sound was present.

Several explanations were proposed. Some suggested geological causes—minor seismic activity, underground water movement, or natural gas flows beneath the earth. Others pointed to industrial sources, such as distant machinery, power lines, pipelines, or communication systems emitting low-frequency noise.

More speculative theories involved military technology, including extremely low-frequency (ELF) radio waves used for submarine communication or undisclosed experiments. None could be proven. Each theory explained parts of the experience, but never the whole.

The Question of the Human Brain

Some experts suggested biological or psychological explanations. They proposed that the hum might be a form of tinnitus or an internal auditory phenomenon. But this explanation also fell short. Many who heard the hum had normal hearing tests. Some described the sound as external, not internal, and reported feeling vibrations rather than hearing a tone.

Others suggested environmental resonance—wind moving through the Rio Grande Gorge, interacting with volcanic rock formations in ways that create low-frequency sound. Again, plausible, but unconfirmed.

One fact remained consistent: only a small percentage of people—estimated at around 2 percent of the population—could hear the hum. This selectivity made it extremely difficult to study objectively and even harder to explain socially.

A Mystery That Does Not Explode

The Taos Hum is not remembered for destruction, violence, or loss of life. It did not flatten buildings or flood streets. Instead, it unsettled daily life in a quieter, more intimate way. It entered bedrooms, thoughts, and moments of silence. It challenged the assumption that reality is shared equally by all.

The hum did not demand fear. It demanded attention. And that, over time, can be just as disturbing.

Living With the Unanswered

Today, the Taos Hum continues. Some residents still hear it. Others never have. No definitive explanation has replaced uncertainty. The mystery remains gentle, persistent, and unresolved.

It reminds us that not all mysteries arrive with force. Some do not shout or destroy. Some simply stay, humming softly through years and generations, asking questions without raising their voice.

And in that quiet persistence, they leave the human mind to sit with uncertainty—
listening,
waiting,
wondering.

Chapter 26

The Unexpected Atom Bomb

"There are moments when a single second changes how people understand safety forever." — Rebecca Solnit

A Normal Morning That Never Returned

On the morning of December 6, 1917, Halifax Harbour looked like it always had. Ships moved slowly through the narrow channel. Dockworkers followed routine habits. The city was alive with ordinary movement. Halifax was one of the busiest ports in the world at the time, a crucial link in the Allied war effort during World War I. Crowded harbours, military supplies, and constant traffic had become normal.

Normal felt safe.

That belief lasted only a few minutes.

A Collision That Should Have Meant Little

Ships collide. It is not unusual. It is rarely catastrophic. That is why what followed was so difficult for the human mind to accept.

The Norwegian vessel SS Imo, empty and heading out to collect relief supplies for Belgium, entered the wrong side of the harbour channel to avoid another ship. At the same time, the French cargo ship SS Mont-Blanc was entering the harbour, heavily loaded with explosives—picric acid, TNT, gun cotton, and barrels of benzol, a highly flammable fuel.

Warning whistles were exchanged. Engines were reversed. But instead of avoiding each other, the bow of the Imo struck the Mont-Blanc.

Sparks flew.

That was all it took.

Fire Before Understanding

Barrels of benzol spilled onto the deck of the Mont-Blanc and ignited instantly. Flames climbed the ship's sides. Thick black smoke rose into the sky. The burning vessel drifted toward the Halifax shoreline.

People gathered to watch.

No alarms rang. No sirens warned the city. Very few understood what the ship carried. The idea that a burning ship could destroy a city was unthinkable. Fires happened. They were fought. This one looked no different.

For about seventeen minutes, Halifax watched without knowing.

The Second That Changed Everything

At 9:04 a.m., the Mont-Blanc detonated.

The explosion released an energy estimated at nearly 3 kilotons of TNT, making it the largest man-made explosion in history before the atomic age. The blast vaporized the ship. A massive shockwave flattened Halifax's north end. Buildings collapsed. Steel bent. Windows shattered miles away. A tsunami surged across the harbour.

Nearly 2,000 people were killed. Over 9,000 were injured, many blinded by flying glass. Entire neighbourhoods vanished. Families were erased in seconds.

And then—silence.

When the Familiar Becomes Lethal

What made the Halifax Explosion so psychologically devastating was not only its size, but its source. Ships were symbols of trade, work, and routine. Harbours were places of livelihood. A collision sounded small, almost harmless.

Yet from that familiar moment came unimaginable destruction.

The human mind expects danger to announce itself—with storms, enemies, or warning signs. Halifax received none. Safety failed quietly, through routine decisions and ordinary errors. That realization shattered more than buildings. It shattered trust.

A City Changed Forever

The explosion reshaped Halifax physically and emotionally. Thousands were left homeless in winter. Relief efforts poured in from across Canada and the United States. Boston's aid became legendary, forming a bond remembered to this day.

Investigations followed. Blame was debated. Responsibility was shared between human error, wartime pressure, poor communication, and dangerous cargo moving through civilian space. No single villain could carry the weight of what had happened.

And that, too, was unsettling.

The Psychological Scar

Events like Halifax change how societies think about risk. They teach a hard lesson: safety is not guaranteed by routine. Systems we trust can fail suddenly. Ordinary actions can lead to irreversible outcomes.

Such knowledge creates fear, but also humility. It forces people to recognize how closely life is tied to invisible structures—rules, coordination, awareness—and how fragile those structures can be.

What Halifax Left Behind

The Halifax Explosion remains fixed in history not only because of its power, but because of its meaning. It revealed

how disasters do not always come from malice or intention. Sometimes they grow quietly, from traffic, habit, and assumption.

A single mistake, a familiar setting, one irreversible second.

And afterward, the human mind is left to carry the weight of understanding what can never be undone.

Chapter 27

Phantom Fear

"Fear is the mind-killer." — Frank Herbert

A Town Already on Edge

In 1944, Mattoon, Illinois was a quiet town, but its calm was thin. The world was at war. Many men were far from home. Radios carried daily reports of death and destruction. Nights felt heavier, filled with waiting and worry. People slept lightly, already tense, even before anything strange began.

Fear did not arrive suddenly. It was already in the air.

The First Night

On the warm night of August 31, 1944, Urban Raef woke abruptly. A sweet, sickening smell filled his home. Soon his body reacted. He felt weak, nauseated, and began to vomit. His wife experienced the same thing—a burning in her throat and a strange heaviness in her legs, as if strength was slowly draining away.

No intruder was seen. No sound was heard. Only the smell remained.

Fear Finds a Shape

The very next night, September 1, another home reported the same experience. Aline Kearney awoke with that same sweet odor in her bedroom. By morning, she felt something terrifying—her legs would not move properly for a short time. Her mouth was dry and swollen. Her body felt unfamiliar, as if it no longer belonged to her.

That evening, her husband Bert noticed a tall, thin figure outside their window, dressed in dark clothing and wearing a tight cap. When he ran outside, the figure vanished into the night.

Now fear had a face.

A Phantom Is Born

Reports spread quickly. Dozens of people described the same pattern: a strange smell, followed by nausea, burning sensations, dry mouths, and temporary weakness or paralysis. Some claimed to find footprints under windows. Others discovered scraps of cloth nearby.

The town gave the fear a name: The Mad Gasser of Mattoon. Some called him the Anesthetic Prowler. Others whispered Phantom Anesthetist. A name made the fear feel real—and unstoppable.

A Town on Watch

These were wartime days. People already feared poison gas, enemy agents, and invisible threats. Every unfamiliar smell felt dangerous. Every shadow looked suspicious. Families locked doors, slept with lights on, and watched through curtains. Armed neighborhood patrols formed, walking the streets with clubs, shotguns, and trembling nerves.

Police investigated repeatedly. Later, even the FBI became involved. Yet no clear evidence appeared. No confirmed gas. No captured attacker. No proof.

Only fear.

When the Mind Takes Over

Under prolonged stress, the human mind becomes sensitive—too sensitive. Normal sensations feel threatening. Fatigue feels like illness. Dry air feels like poison. What may have begun as a few real physical reactions—possibly from industrial fumes—grew into something larger.

Newspaper headlines amplified the fear. Neighbors repeated stories. Anxiety spread faster than any prowler could move. People began to feel symptoms even before smelling anything at all.

Fear learned how to travel without a body.

The Silence After

By mid-September, officials suggested other explanations: chemical fumes from a nearby factory, shifting winds, or the powerful force of collective hysteria. Slowly, the reports faded. The nights grew quiet again. The Mad Gasser disappeared as silently as he had arrived.

No one was arrested. No attacker was ever proven to exist.

The Real Lesson

The mystery of Mattoon remains unsolved, but its meaning is clear. It shows how fear, when fed by war, loneliness, and uncertainty, can enter the body itself. How the unseen can feel real enough to harm. How the mind, under strain, can turn ordinary sensations into danger.

And perhaps the deepest truth the town learned was this: sometimes the most frightening visitor does not come through the window, but rises quietly from within the human mind itself.

Chapter 28

The Dancing Mania

"The mind and body are not separate. What affects one, affects the other." — Hippocrates

A Quiet Town, An Unquiet Year

In the year 1374, something strange settled over Aachen, a small and quiet town of the old world. Life there followed familiar rhythms—work at dawn, prayer at dusk, seasons that came and went without surprise. People knew hardship, but it was hardship they could name and endure. Then, without warning, something slipped beyond those boundaries.

It did not arrive with noise or ceremony. It arrived through the body.

The Dance Without Music

A few people began to move. Not in joy. Not to song. There was no festival, no drum, no reason anyone could explain. Their feet struck the ground again and again. Arms swung as if guided by invisible hands. Faces tightened with pain, not pleasure. And yet, they could not stop.

What began with a handful soon drew many more. Men and women, young and old, filled streets and open squares, moving together in a rhythm no one had chosen. Hours passed. Then days. Bodies weakened, but the motion continued. Some collapsed, only to rise and begin again. Others wept as they danced, terrified by the loss of control.

There was still no music. Only movement.

When the Mind Overflows

The people of Aachen were not strangers to fear. Hunger lingered. Disease had not long loosened its grip. Memories of death and loss lived close to the skin. Worry had no safe place to rest. And when the mind can no longer hold such weight, it sometimes hands the burden to the body.

This was not an isolated moment. Stories had already reached Aachen from Strasbourg, where people had danced in the same helpless way. Now Aachen followed, as if the fear itself had learned how to travel.

No one understood it then.

Fear That Learned to Move

Some called it punishment from God. Others whispered of poisoned blood or demonic touch. But with distance and time, a clearer picture emerges. This was shared suffering, passing quietly from one person to another. Fear spread. Exhaustion spread. And soon, the movement spread as well.

When one body trembles, another begins to mirror it. When one person loses control, others feel the pull. In moments of deep strain, emotion becomes contagious. Pain seeks company. The body speaks when words fail.

Belief, Stress, and Contagion

Faith shaped how people understood what they saw. Many believed saints such as St. John or St. Vitus had cursed the dancers. Others feared possession. These beliefs did not calm the fear—they fed it. The more people believed the dancing was unavoidable, the more tightly it took hold.

Some later suggested poisoned rye, tainted by ergot fungus, as the cause. Others pointed to illnesses like epilepsy or encephalitis. While these ideas explain parts of the behavior, none fully account for the way the dancing spread through communities, following roads, trade routes, and shared stories.

What fits most closely is the weight of collective stress. Famine, recurring plagues, floods, and deep uncertainty had worn people thin. The body became a release, an escape, a shared trance where suffering could finally move.

The Cost of Misunderstanding

Authorities tried to respond, but their efforts often worsened the pain. Some isolated the dancers. Others forced them to keep dancing, believing exhaustion would bring healing. Many collapsed from injury or strain. A few never rose again.

The movement eventually faded, but it left behind no clear cure—only questions.

What the Dance Still Tells Us

The Dancing Mania of Aachen did not leave records of answers. It left a lesson. It showed how closely people are bound to one another, not only in joy, but in distress. It revealed how fear can become physical, how belief can shape the body, and how suffering can learn to travel through изменений no one intends.

This is not only a story of madness. It is a quiet reminder. When life grows too heavy, the human mind sometimes finds strange ways to speak—through trembling feet, aching muscles, and movements no one ever chose.

Chapter 29

Ghosts in the Courtroom

"Where fear rules, reason sleeps." — Voltaire

A Village Under a Long Shadow

In the winter of 1692, Salem was a place shaped by hard work, strict faith, and quiet tension. The snow had melted, yet a cold shadow seemed to linger over the village. Life moved by rigid rules, and belief filled the spaces where certainty failed. It was in this uneasy stillness that something strange began inside the home of the village minister, Samuel Parris.

His young daughter, Betty, and his niece, Abigail Williams, started to twist and tremble without warning. Their bodies bent into unnatural shapes. They cried out in pain, claiming unseen hands were pinching and stabbing them. Their voices grew wild and broken, as if someone else were speaking through them. What frightened the village most was not just their suffering, but the fact that no one could see its cause.

When Fear Finds a Name

A doctor was called. He examined the girls and found no illness of the body. Unable to explain what he saw, he offered a single, chilling conclusion: an evil hand was at work.

That sentence changed everything.

Once spoken, it took root in a community already trained to believe in unseen threats. Fear moved quickly. Other girls soon began to show the same fits. They screamed, crawled beneath furniture, and stared at empty corners with wide, terrified eyes. When asked who was hurting them, they named three women who already lived at the edges of the village's trust.

Tituba, the enslaved woman from the Caribbean, was different in language and skin, and she told stories the children found strange and exciting. Sarah Good was poor, homeless, and often angry. Sarah Osborne kept to herself and rarely came to church. They were not powerful, protected, or loved. They were easy to accuse.

Ghosts in the Courtroom

When the women were brought before the court, the room was packed with fear and anger. As soon as the accused entered, the girls collapsed into violent fits, screaming that invisible spirits were attacking them. These spirits, they claimed, belonged to the women standing before them.

This idea, known as spectral evidence, was accepted as truth. A person's unseen ghost could be used as proof of guilt. It was a ghost story spoken under oath, and the court believed it.

A Confession That Fed the Fire

Under terror and pressure, Tituba confessed. She spoke of dark animals, secret meetings, and a tall man who served the devil. Her words were vivid and frightening. Instead of calming the village, they deepened the panic. If she was telling the truth, then evil was not limited to three women. It was everywhere, hidden behind familiar faces.

Accusations spread like fire. Old quarrels, jealousies, and grudges rose to the surface. A harsh word, a disagreement, or a moment of bad luck could turn into an accusation. Even the respected were not spared. Martha Corey questioned the girls' claims and was quickly named a witch. Her husband, Giles Corey, defended her and soon found himself accused as well.

Fear as a Machine

The jails filled with innocent people. A special court was created, and it accepted the girls' visions as solid proof. Denial was taken as guilt. Confession, especially if it included naming others, could save a life. Fear fed fear, and the system sustained itself.

Some people broke and confessed to lies in order to survive. Others refused. Rebecca Nurse, a gentle and deeply religious grandmother, chose truth over safety and walked calmly toward death. Giles Corey chose a different path. When brought to trial, he refused to speak, knowing any answer would condemn him. For his silence, he was punished by having heavy stones placed upon his body until he was crushed to death. His final words, spoken through pain, were said to be, “More weight.” He died so his land would remain with his sons.

When the Fever Finally Broke

By the time the governor ended the trials and banned spectral evidence, twenty people were dead. Nineteen were hanged. One was pressed beneath stones. Then, almost as suddenly as it had begun, the madness faded.

Salem was left in silence.

Years later, the courts admitted their error. Trials were declared unlawful. One judge, Samuel Sewall, publicly confessed his guilt and asked for forgiveness. Ann Putnam Jr., one of the main accusers, later admitted her role and expressed deep remorse. The village tried to heal, but the memory never left.

What Salem Truly Reveals

The story of Salem is not a story about witches. It is a story about fear. It grew from religious extremism, political and economic conflict, old family feuds, war-related trauma, and the need to blame someone when life felt unbearable.

Outsiders, the poor, the elderly, and the powerless became vessels for the community's anxiety.

This was mass hysteria shaped by belief and power, not evidence or reason.

Salem teaches us that when fear is given authority, it can turn neighbours into enemies and doubt into certainty. The ghosts they feared were not hiding in the woods or floating through courtrooms. They were born inside human minds, fed by suspicion, and made real by belief.

The true haunting of Salem was not supernatural. It was human.

Chapter 30

Devil's Verdict

"The greatest tragedy is not when belief and science disagree, but when neither is willing to let compassion lead." — Carl Jung

A Quiet Beginning

In the quiet towns of Germany during the 1960s, a young girl named Anneliese Michel grew up in a home shaped by discipline, devotion, and faith. She was thoughtful, intelligent, and deeply religious, attending church often and dreaming of a future as a schoolteacher. Her life appeared ordinary, even hopeful, until she was sixteen years old, when something within her began to break.

She started suffering violent seizures. Her body stiffened without warning, her consciousness slipping away as if her mind had fled. Doctors examined her and gave the condition a name: epilepsy, a disorder of the brain. Later, as her behavior changed, they added further diagnoses, including depression and psychosis. Medicine offered explanations and treatment, but it did not offer peace.

When Illness Became Meaning

For Anneliese and her deeply religious family, the medical explanation felt incomplete. During her seizures, she reported seeing terrifying faces and hearing voices filled with hatred and blasphemy. Sacred images repelled her. Prayer, once a comfort, became a battlefield. To her parents, and eventually to Anneliese herself, these were not symptoms. They were signs.

Her suffering began to take on meaning. She came to believe she was chosen to endure pain for a higher purpose. Food felt impure. Comfort felt undeserved. She slept on stone floors, denied herself nourishment, and punished her body in acts she believed were holy. Pain, to her, was not an enemy. It was proof.

She moved back and forth between hospitals and churches. Psychiatrists adjusted medications and spoke of illness. Priests listened and spoke of possession. Slowly, the medical voice grew quieter, and the spiritual one grew louder.

The Rituals Begin

In 1975, after long deliberation, the local bishop granted permission for an exorcism. Two priests, Theobald S. and Ernst A., were assigned to her case. What followed was not a single ritual, but sixty-seven exorcisms, carried out over nearly ten months.

These sessions were long and physically exhausting. They were filled with shouting, prayer, resistance, and fear. Anneliese screamed, cursed, barked like an animal, and recoiled from holy objects. She crawled under furniture, tore at her clothes, and begged for relief. The priests believed they were confronting not one presence, but several, naming figures such as Lucifer, Judas, Nero, and Cain. Many of these sessions were recorded on tape, leaving behind haunting evidence of her torment.

Through it all, Anneliese continued to refuse food and water. Her parents and the priests, convinced they were fighting for her soul, did not intervene. They did not force nourishment. They did not return her to intensive medical care. Suffering, they believed, was part of salvation.

A Body That Could No Longer Endure

By the summer of 1976, Anneliese Michel was dying. Her body had been reduced to bone and skin. She weighed only sixty-eight pounds. Her knees were broken from endless praying. She was severely dehydrated, malnourished, and suffering from pneumonia.

On July 1st, after one final exorcism, she collapsed. Her heart, weakened by starvation, stopped. She was twenty-three years old.

Judgment on Earth

When authorities examined her body, they saw not a miracle delayed, but a death caused by neglect. The state brought charges of negligent homicide against her parents and the two priests. The trial that followed became a public reckoning.

In the courtroom, the same battle that had consumed Anneliese played out again. The prosecution spoke in the language of medicine: epilepsy, psychosis, starvation, dehydration. The defense spoke in the language of faith: possession, sacrifice, divine struggle. The exorcism tapes were played aloud. One voice declared, chillingly, "Anneliese must die."

The court ruled that belief did not excuse responsibility. All four were found guilty and given suspended sentences. The judgment was clear: the duty to preserve life could not be abandoned, even in the name of saving a soul.

What Her Story Leaves Behind

The story of Anneliese Michel is not a tale of demons. It is a story of collision. Two powerful systems—faith and medicine—stood facing one another, each convinced of its truth, neither willing to yield. In that conflict, a young woman disappeared.

Her grave in Klingenberg has since become a place of pilgrimage for some and a warning for others. To believers, she remains a martyr. To medicine, she is a victim of untreated illness. To history, she is something more painful still: a reminder of what happens when certainty hardens and compassion is lost.

Anneliese was not lost to possession alone, nor to illness alone. She was lost in the space between them, where

argument replaced care, and where fighting for a soul meant forgetting the fragile human being who carried it.

Chapter 31

Another American Foolishness

"The most frightening stories are the ones we tell ourselves." — Walter Lippmann

A Familiar Voice in the Dark

On the evening of October 30, 1938, as daylight faded and families settled into their homes, millions of Americans did what felt natural and safe. They gathered around the radio. It was the trusted voice in the living room, a steady companion that brought music, news, and reassurance into ordinary lives.

That night, on the CBS network, a program called *The Mercury Theatre on the Air* began. Its host was a young and gifted actor named Orson Welles. At the start, an announcement explained that the broadcast would be a dramatic adaptation of H. G. Wells's *The War of the Worlds.* Then the music played—gentle dance tunes, familiar and calming.

And then, the music stopped.

News That Felt Too Real

The interruption came in the form of a news bulletin. A reporter spoke of strange explosions observed on the surface of Mars. Moments later, another update followed. A flaming object, he said, had crashed into a farm in Grovers Mill, New Jersey.

Listeners heard the reporter describe the scene in breathless detail. A metallic cylinder lay in a crater. Its top began to unscrew. From inside came a disturbing hissing sound. Then the reporter screamed as something rose into view—a leathery, tentacled creature. His voice cut off suddenly.

More bulletins followed, growing faster and more chaotic. Towering Martian machines were advancing. A heat-ray was burning towns to ash. The army was mobilizing. New York City was threatened. The broadcast mirrored the exact tone and structure of real emergency news. It did not feel like fiction. It felt immediate. It felt official.

For many listeners who had tuned in late and missed the opening disclaimer, this was not a radio play. It was history unfolding in real time.

When Imagination Took Command

Across parts of the country, fear took hold. In New Jersey, people ran into the streets with wet towels pressed to their faces, convinced poison gas was spreading. Police stations were flooded with frantic citizens claiming to have heard presidential emergency announcements. Families packed their cars and fled with whatever they could carry. Telephone lines collapsed under the weight of panic.

The terror was genuine. People were not pretending. Their bodies reacted as if the threat were real.

Yet later examination showed that the panic was not as widespread as newspapers suggested. The program aired against a far more popular show on another network, and most listeners either did not hear it or understood it was fiction. Still, for those who believed, the experience was overwhelming. The radio, a device they trusted completely, had betrayed them with a story delivered in the voice of authority.

After the Silence

Inside the studio, Orson Welles and his cast were stunned. They had intended a clever Halloween performance, not national alarm. At the end of the broadcast, Welles stepped out of character and reassured listeners, comparing the show to "dressing up in a sheet and saying, 'Boo.'"

The following day, headlines shouted about mass hysteria. Welles, shaken and worried for his future, addressed the press with humility and calm. He apologized sincerely, yet also seemed quietly astonished by what had happened. "We frightened the devil out of a few people," he said, "but I think they'll get over it."

They did.

What That Night Revealed

The panic faded, but the story endured. It became part of American folklore, retold not as a tale of foolishness, but as a lesson in human psychology. It revealed how deeply people trusted the sound of an authoritative voice, how powerfully imagination could fill the gaps when fear was given just enough detail to grow.

That night was not really about Martians. It was about belief. About how easily the boundary between story and reality can dissolve when we are listening alone in the dark. For one unforgettable hour, an entire nation learned how quickly the mind can turn sound into certainty, and fiction into truth.

Chapter 32

The Stinking City

"Sometimes, a city must smell its own truth before it can see its own future." — Edwin Chadwick

When a River Became a Warning

Let us return to London in the summer of 1858, a city at the height of its power. It was the capital of an empire, loud with factories, crowded with ambition, and alive with progress. Through its center flowed the River Thames, a wide, muddy ribbon that had carried trade, history, and pride for centuries.

By that year, however, the Thames was no longer truly a river. It had become something darker.

For decades, London had poured its waste into the water. Every household drain, every overflowing cesspit, every factory outlet emptied directly into the river. As the city's population exploded, the Thames quietly absorbed it all. By the middle of the nineteenth century, it had become London's open sewer.

The Summer That Changed Everything

Then came the heat.

In 1858, a relentless summer sun settled over the city. Day after day, the temperature rose. The river slowed and thickened, its surface dark and lifeless. What lay beneath began to rot.

And the smell rose.

It was not merely unpleasant. It was overpowering. A choking, eye-watering stench of human waste and decay that clung to clothes, burned the throat, and filled the lungs. The city named it The Great Stink, and the name did not exaggerate. The odor crept through streets and homes, refusing to be ignored.

Its most important victim stood directly on the riverbank.

Power Meets Reality

The Houses of Parliament, symbols of reason and authority, were no match for the river. Members tried to continue their work, but the stench forced itself inside. Curtains were soaked in chloride of lime and hung over windows in desperate attempts to block the smell. It failed. The foul air poured through the chambers like a living thing.

Debates were interrupted. Sessions were abandoned. Lawmakers pressed handkerchiefs to their faces and fled the room. The river had reached the seat of power, and it was speaking in a language no one could dismiss.

This was no longer an abstract problem. It could not be delayed, denied, or ignored. It was in their noses, their throats, and their lungs.

Action at Last

In a matter of days, years of argument collapsed. The same politicians who had long hesitated over the cost of reform moved with astonishing speed. Emergency legislation was passed. Authority and funding were granted to an engineer who had already seen the solution clearly: Joseph Bazalgette.

Bazalgette's vision was bold and precise. He designed a vast network of underground sewers—huge, egg-shaped brick tunnels that ran for miles along both sides of the Thames. These intercepting sewers would catch waste before it reached the river and carry it far downstream. Powerful pumping stations, built like monuments, lifted sewage and kept it moving.

It was the largest civil engineering project the world had ever seen.

The City Beneath the City

For years, London was torn open. Streets disappeared. Brick by brick, an unseen city grew beneath the visible one. When the system was complete, something remarkable happened.

The river began to change.

The stench faded. The water slowly cleared. Cholera outbreaks, long blamed on foul air under the miasma theory, began to disappear—though unknowingly, it was clean water that saved lives. Bazalgette's work did more than end a smell. It transformed public health and protected generations to come.

What the Smell Taught London

The Great Stink was not a grand moral awakening. It was not a triumph of data or debate. It was a moment when reality became unbearable.

London did not act because of reports or charts. It acted because the truth could no longer be held at a distance. The city was forced to confront itself through the most basic of human senses. The river held up a mirror, and the reflection could not be denied.

That is the quiet lesson of 1858. Sometimes, progress does not begin with vision or virtue. Sometimes, it begins with discomfort. With a collective gasp. With the simple realization that living as we are has become impossible.

And so, a great and dirty city finally cleaned itself—not because it wanted to, but because it had no other choice.

Chapter 33

Fish from Sky

"The world is stranger than our certainty allows." — J. B. S. Haldane

An Ordinary Day, Until It Wasn't

In the autumn of 1947, something quietly unsettling happened in a small town in Louisiana called Marksville. It was not a place where history usually paused. Life moved at a gentle pace, shaped by routine, weather, and familiarity.

That day, the weather felt unremarkable. The sky was grey. The air was damp. A light storm drifted through, nothing fierce enough to inspire fear. People went about their business, trusting the sky to behave as it always had.

Then the ordinary world slipped.

The Impossible Falls

Fish began to fall from the sky.

Not a single fish, not a trick of the eye, but many—small fish, some still moving, scattered across streets and yards. They fell over a long stretch of land, enough for people in different parts of town to witness the same strange sight.

There was no roar of wind, no dramatic funnel cloud, no warning. Just fish where rain should have been.

People stopped. They stared. They pointed. Some bent down to touch the evidence, as if their hands might confirm what their minds refused to accept. The sea, it seemed, had briefly forgotten its place.

When Meaning Breaks Down

Storms already unsettle the human mind. They remind us that control is fragile. But this was something else. Rain follows rules. Fish do not belong in clouds.

When nature breaks its own patterns, fear does not always arrive as panic. Sometimes it comes as silence. As confusion. As a quiet sense that something fundamental has been disturbed.

Some people laughed nervously. Others felt awe. A few felt genuine unease. When the world behaves in ways we cannot explain, it touches something ancient inside us—the knowledge that certainty is an illusion.

The Name That Remained

The event came to be remembered as the Marksville Fish Rain of 1947. Eyewitness accounts were consistent. The fish ranged from a few inches to nearly a foot in length. They were spread across a defined area, ruling out simple accidents or human interference.

There was no immediate explanation that day. Only questions, stories, and the lingering image of fish lying on wet ground beneath a quiet sky.

What Science Suggests

In time, science offered a calm and plausible answer.

Meteorologists believe the fish were lifted from a nearby body of water by a powerful waterspout or strong storm updraft. A waterspout is a rotating column of air over water, capable of pulling up fish along with large volumes of spray.

The process is simple, though it feels unbelievable. The fish are drawn upward, carried along by winds, and then released when the storm weakens. Gravity does the rest.

No dramatic funnel was recorded that day, but waterspouts can form briefly and vanish without leaving clear traces. The explanation fits the facts, even if it fails to erase the wonder.

What People Remember

Yet science does not fully account for what stayed with those who witnessed it.

What lingered was not the fish themselves, but the feeling—the moment when the sky betrayed expectation. When the border between sea and air dissolved, and reality felt thin.

For those who saw it, the memory remained like the smell after rain, sharp and unforgettable. A reminder that the world does not owe us predictability. That beneath our

habits and explanations, nature still holds the power to surprise.

Sometimes, the sky gives back the sea. And for a brief moment, we are reminded how little we truly command, and how much we merely assume.

Chapter 34

The Great Greek Fire

"Sometimes the best defense is not a stronger wall, but a mystery your enemy cannot face." — Sun Tzu

A City That Learned to Survive

Constantinople was more than a city. It was the heart of an empire, shining with faith, wealth, and power. Its walls were legendary, its position unmatched, standing where Europe and Asia met. Yet for all its strength, the Byzantine Empire lived under constant threat. For centuries, enemies gathered at its gates and sailed toward its harbours, certain that time would eventually bring the city down.

In its darkest hours, Byzantium did not rely only on stone and soldiers. It relied on a secret.

They called it Liquid Fire. The world would remember it as Greek Fire.

The Man Who Brought the Flame

The story begins with a man named Kallinikos, a Syrian architect and engineer. As Arab armies swept across the eastern lands, he fled to Constantinople, carrying with him knowledge that would change history. He brought not an army, but an idea—a terrible mixture that could turn fire itself into a weapon of terror.

In the year 678, a vast Arab fleet sailed confidently into the Bosporus Strait, certain the city would finally fall. Byzantine ships moved to meet them, ordinary in shape, unremarkable at first glance. Then something unexpected appeared.

From the prows of the ships extended bronze tubes, shaped like the heads of lions or dragons.

Fire That Defied the Sea

With a thunderous roar, liquid flame burst from the bronze mouths. It arced through the air and struck the enemy ships. This was no ordinary fire. It clung to wood and sail, spreading like a living thing. It burned on the surface of the water, turning the sea itself into fire.

The sailors panicked. Water could not save them. Some said it only fed the flames. Men jumped overboard, only to find the waves burning beneath them. Within moments, the proud fleet was chaos. Ships burned. Crews vanished. The sea glowed with fire.

Constantinople was saved.

The Secret Within the Secret

Greek Fire was more than a weapon. It was a mystery carefully protected by the state. Its exact formula was known only to the emperor and a single family of specialists, often believed to be descended from Kallinikos himself. It was never written down. It was whispered, memorized, and mixed in hidden workshops deep within the palace.

Historians believe the substance likely included naphtha, a crude form of petroleum, mixed with pine resin and sulfur. A key element may have been quicklime, which reacts violently with water, creating intense heat. This reaction could explain why the fire seemed to ignite on contact with the sea and why water failed to extinguish it.

But the liquid alone was not enough.

A Weapon of Engineering and Fear

The true brilliance of Greek Fire lay in its delivery. The Byzantines had designed pressurized siphons that could spray the burning liquid in a continuous stream. Mounted on ships, these devices turned naval battles into nightmares. It was, in effect, a medieval flamethrower.

The sound, the smoke, and the unstoppable flames created terror far beyond physical destruction. To face a Byzantine warship was to face something monstrous, a machine that breathed fire like a dragon from legend. Often, the fear alone was enough to break enemy formations before battle truly began.

The Flame That Vanished

For centuries, Greek Fire protected the empire. It helped repel repeated sieges and preserved Constantinople long after other ancient powers had fallen. But secrets, like empires, do not last forever.

When Constantinople finally fell to the Ottomans in 1453, the knowledge of Greek Fire disappeared with it. Perhaps the last man who knew the full recipe died in the final siege. Since then, scholars and chemists have tried to recreate it. They can make substances that burn on water, but none fully match the ancient descriptions of that sticky, roaring, unquenchable flame.

The fire that saved an empire became a legend.

What Greek Fire Truly Was

Greek Fire teaches a quiet lesson about power. The Byzantines' greatest weapon was not just fire, but mystery. It was fear made physical, knowledge turned into silence, and ingenuity guarded with absolute care.

In the end, Greek Fire did not merely burn ships. It burned itself into history, then vanished, leaving only stories and echoes. It reminds us that some forms of knowledge are so powerful they can shape centuries—and so fragile they can disappear forever, like fire on water, leaving nothing behind but smoke and memory.

Understood. Below is the revised version with all such list-style, single-line sentences converted into continuous, flowing prose, while preserving clarity, tone, and meaning.

Chapter 35

Travelling Lie

"A lie can travel halfway around the world while the truth is still putting on its shoes." — Mark Twain

Before the Internet Learned to Whisper

Long before tweets, posts, or algorithms shaped public opinion, another kind of network was already at work. It hummed through radio waves, rattled across teletype machines, and hid inside official-looking envelopes. This was the Cold War, a conflict fought as much with ideas as with weapons, where victory depended on belief as much as territory.

To fight this invisible war, intelligence agencies learned a crucial lesson: influencing human thought did not always require a visible human face. A voice without a clear owner, a document without a traceable source, or the illusion of many people speaking at once could be just as powerful.

Voices from Nowhere

Across Europe, Asia, and Africa, strange radio stations began appearing on shortwave dials. They were not the authoritative voices of established broadcasters like the BBC or Radio Moscow. These signals felt smaller and stranger, slipping between frequencies and appearing without warning.

A listener might hear familiar Western music, ordinary and comforting, before it was suddenly interrupted by an urgent news bulletin. The voice would report protests that had never occurred, scandals that did not exist, or conflicts hidden from public view. The tone was calm, confident, and designed to sound credible.

Some of these stations were openly Western-backed, such as Radio Free Europe and Radio Liberty, funded by the CIA to bypass censorship behind the Iron Curtain. Others were darker and more secretive, operating as covert "black" stations with no declared origin. They broadcast briefly, changed frequencies, and vanished, leaving listeners uncertain whether they had heard truth or illusion.

The Soviet Union responded in kind. Stations like Radio Peace and Progress presented themselves as the voices of ordinary, peace-loving citizens while quietly advancing state narratives to foreign audiences. The result was a twilight zone of information, where listeners could no longer be sure who was speaking or why.

Documents That Lied Convincingly

The Soviet intelligence services refined another weapon that did not rely on sound, but on paper. They called these efforts "active measures," a broad system of political warfare designed to influence opinion without direct confrontation.

KGB operatives became experts in forgery, creating letters, military reports, and government memoranda that appeared authentic even to trained eyes. These documents were then carefully leaked to sympathetic journalists, diplomats, or activist groups. One of the most infamous campaigns, known as Operation INFEKTION, spread the false claim that the AIDS virus had been engineered by the U.S. military. The aim was not immediate belief, but lingering doubt. If one official document could be fake, then perhaps all of them were.

When People Became the Network

Before automation existed, human beings filled its role. Intelligence agencies recruited writers, students, emigrés, and journalists and asked them to perform a simple task: write letters, again and again.

These letters were sent to newspaper editors, international organizations, and political offices. Each appeared personal and sincere, signed with a different name, yet all echoed the same approved message. A single individual, writing under many identities, could create the impression of a growing public movement. It was consensus manufactured through repetition, not conviction, and it worked because it looked organic.

Why the Illusion Worked

The effectiveness of these methods lay in human psychology. People are naturally drawn to what appears popular or widely accepted. When the same idea appears repeatedly, voiced by many apparent sources, it feels safer to agree than to question.

A reader in Madrid or New Delhi, encountering multiple letters or reports expressing the same outrage, might assume the sentiment reflected genuine public opinion. The narrative did not need evidence. It only needed familiarity. Through repetition and emotional framing, doubt became acceptance.

The Inheritance of the Digital Age

These Cold War techniques lacked the speed and scale of modern digital systems, but they established the principles that now dominate online disinformation. They relied on anonymity and false attribution, emotional manipulation rather than evidence, repetition to simulate truth, and the quiet hijacking of trusted communication channels.

Information itself became the battlefield. Success no longer required destroying an enemy's forces, but weakening their confidence in reality. The ultimate victory was not silence, but confusion.

The Machine Learns to Haunt

Long before people logged on, these ghosts were already moving through the machine. They whispered through radios, appeared in forged documents, and spoke through dozens of borrowed names. They learned how to make coordinated messages feel spontaneous and sincere.

In doing so, they built the first rough engines of manufactured reality. The digital age did not invent disinformation; it merely automated it. The ghosts never left the machine. They simply learned how to move faster.

Chapter 36

The Sound of Dark Angel

"The human mind is capable of far more than we understand, including suffering that leaves no visible wound." — William James

The Sound That Had No Source

It began quietly in Havana, Cuba, in 2016. American and Canadian diplomats, along with their families, noticed something deeply unsettling. They would be resting in a hotel room or sitting at home when a sound seemed to find them. It was sharp and grating, sometimes like a piercing screech, sometimes like a pressure moving through the skull rather than entering the ears. There was no speaker, no machine, no clear direction. The sound felt personal, as if it had chosen its listener.

When the Body Followed the Sound

Soon, the sound was followed by pain. Intense headaches struck without warning. Dizziness made rooms tilt and floors feel unsteady. A ringing settled into the ears and refused to fade. Some felt nauseous; others struggled to think clearly or remember simple words. Vision blurred. Balance failed. What frightened many was not only the pain, but its suddenness. It felt like an attack.

For some, the symptoms lingered for months. Fatigue became constant. Sleep fractured. A heavy mental fog settled in, making ordinary life difficult. Whatever this was, it was real, and it was disabling.

A Mystery That Traveled

What made the fear grow was that Havana was not the end of the story. Similar reports surfaced in China, Germany, Austria, Vietnam, and even quiet neighborhoods near Washington, D.C. A senior U.S. defense official experienced symptoms during a NATO summit in Lithuania. By some estimates, hundreds of diplomats, intelligence officers, and family members were affected across the world.

Different places. Different buildings. The same pattern.

A sound, followed by suffering, with no visible cause.

The Search for an Enemy

The world demanded an explanation, and the first answer was the most frightening. Perhaps this was a new kind of weapon. Experts spoke of directed energy, such as pulsed microwaves, focused precisely into rooms. Attention turned toward foreign adversaries, especially Russia, long rumored to be researching "psychotronic" weapons.

This theory gave shape to fear. An invisible assault is easier to bear when it has a name and an enemy.

When the Evidence Refused to Agree

Years of investigation followed. In 2023, after extensive review, the U.S. intelligence community reached a conclusion that surprised many. Seven agencies stated it was highly unlikely that a foreign adversary was responsible. They found no consistent forensic evidence, no clear signature of a weapon, and no proof that an attack had taken place. Some intelligence even suggested that other nations were themselves puzzled by the accusations.

"Havana Syndrome," the report noted, was not a single medical discovery, but a broad label. It gathered many symptoms, stress responses, and environmental factors into one troubling name.

Science Without a Scar

Medical science reached a similar and uncomfortable place. In 2024, the National Institutes of Health completed a nearly five-year study of those affected. Advanced brain scans, blood tests, and cognitive assessments were conducted. The result was paradoxical. There was no evidence of brain injury. No biological marker of damage. No physical trace of an attack.

And yet, the researchers were clear: the suffering was real.

Many participants showed signs of persistent balance disorders, chronic fatigue, post-traumatic stress, and depression. The lead scientist, Dr. Leighton Chan, summarized the finding with care. If something external had occurred, it left no lasting physical evidence that science could detect.

Between Proof and Pain

This created a painful divide. For those affected, the experience was undeniable. Their health had been shattered by something sudden and intrusive. To hear that there was no physical evidence felt, to many, like being told their pain did not matter. Some spoke openly of feeling dismissed or "gaslighted."

On the other side, scientists and analysts could only follow the data before them. That data pointed away from weapons and toward a complex interaction of stress, environment, expectation, and belief.

The Power of Expectation

Some researchers began to look closely at context. The earliest cases were publicly framed as attacks. In high-stress diplomatic and intelligence postings, awareness sharpened. Strange sounds became alarming. Normal sensations felt dangerous. One declassified report even matched a mysterious grating noise heard in Cuba to the mating call of a local cricket.

What sounded like a weapon in one context was, in another, simply an insect.

The Quiet Truth That Remains

And so the mystery endures, not in laboratories or intelligence files, but in the space between perception and proof. Havana Syndrome is not a story of clear villains or simple answers. It is a story of modern fear, where the threat is not a soldier at the gate, but a sound in a quiet room, a pressure in the head, a dread that cannot be photographed or scanned.

It reminds us of an uncomfortable truth. Real pain does not always leave visible scars. The mind, when it believes it is under siege, can wage a war of its own. The wounds it creates are invisible, but they are no less real.

In the end, Havana Syndrome may tell us less about secret weapons and more about the fragile boundary between belief and the body, and how easily that boundary can break when certainty disappears.

Chapter 37

The Alien Radiation

"The most terrifying thing is not what we cannot see, but what we see clearly and are told never existed."
— Albert Camus

A Quiet Road in Texas

On the night of December 29, 1980, the pine forests near Huffman, Texas, were still and dark. A narrow road cut through the trees, carrying little traffic at that hour. One car moved slowly along it, heading home after a late dinner. Inside were three ordinary people: Betty Cash, Vickie Landrum, and Vickie's seven-year-old grandson, Colby. They were tired, relaxed, and thinking of nothing more than sleep.

Nothing about the night suggested danger.

Then the forest lit up.

The Light That Would Not Pass

At first, the light seemed harmless. Bright, steady, and low, it looked like an aircraft approaching a landing strip. They continued driving. But the light returned, closer now, hanging just above the treetops.

Betty slowed the car. Vickie told her to stop.

Above the road hovered something enormous.

They later described it as diamond-shaped, standing upright, its surface dull and metallic, silver against the dark sky. It was as large as a water tower and completely silent. From its flat underside, flames burst downward in a wide cone, roaring like a furnace. Each blast lifted the object slightly upward. When the fire paused, it drifted back down, as if struggling to stay in the air.

The heat rolled over them in waves.

Fire Without Mercy

Betty stepped out of the car, unable to look away. The heat struck her instantly. She would later say it felt as though it was burning her from the inside. Vickie rushed back into the car, shielding Colby, who had begun to cry in terror.

Betty stood frozen until the pain forced her to move. When she reached for the car door, the metal handle scorched her hand. She had to wrap her coat around it to pull the door open.

Inside the car, Vickie braced herself against the dashboard. Her fingers sank into the vinyl as if it were soft clay, leaving a perfect imprint behind.

Then came the sound.

The Circle in the Sky

A deep, rhythmic *thump-thump-thump* filled the air. From the darkness, helicopters emerged—one after another, from every direction. Betty and Vickie later said there were twenty-three of them. They were large, twin-rotor CH-47 Chinooks, some clearly marked United States Air Force.

They formed a tight circle around the burning object, as if escorting it or trying to contain it. Together, the helicopters and the flaming craft moved away, disappearing into the night.

The forest went silent again.

They believed it was over.

When the Body Tells the Truth

The sickness began that same night.

Colby woke screaming for water, burning with fever and vomiting. By morning, all three felt weak and drained. Their skin turned red and painfully sensitive, like severe sunburn. Over the following days, Betty Cash deteriorated rapidly. Blisters formed across her body. Her hair began to fall out in clumps. She became too weak to stand.

On January 3, 1981, she was admitted to a hospital in Houston.

The doctors were alarmed. Betty Cash, they said, showed signs of massive radiation exposure. Her physician, Dr.

Brian McClelland, later described her condition as a textbook case, comparable to someone standing several miles from the center of Hiroshima during the atomic bombing.

Vickie and Colby were also ill. They suffered nausea, skin lesions, and hair loss. Though less severe, their health never fully returned.

Taking the Government to Court

Unlike most people who encounter the unexplained, Betty and Vickie did not retreat into silence. They went to court.

Believing the military helicopters were key to what they had seen, they filed a $20 million lawsuit against the U.S. government. Their case was supported by attorney Peter Gersten and a former NASA investigator. They pointed to the helicopters, the burns, and a disturbing detail: the section of road where the object had hovered was later dug up and removed by men in unmarked trucks.

The government denied everything.

Officials from the Air Force, NASA, and the Army testified under oath that no such craft existed and that no military helicopters were operating over Huffman, Texas, that night. There were no records, no logs, no admissions.

In 1986, the case was dismissed. The judge accepted the official record over the physical suffering of the witnesses.

What Could Not Be Explained Away

With the courtroom closed, the mystery deepened.

Investigators proposed that the object may have been a secret experimental craft, possibly a NASA or military re-entry vehicle using unstable propulsion. Such a system could explain the flames, the extreme heat, and the heavy helicopter escort. A malfunction might have forced it dangerously low over a public road.

Yet one problem refused to disappear.

The medical evidence.

The burns, hair loss, immune damage, and long-term illness were real, documented, and severe. This was not fear. This was physical trauma. Still, no known radiation source could be identified. Some researchers suggested exposure to exotic fuels or propulsion byproducts never publicly acknowledged.

The Cost of Denial

Officially, nothing happened that night.

But bodies do not lie easily.

Betty Cash spent the rest of her life battling recurring cancer and died in 1998. Vickie and Colby lived on with weakened immune systems and the memory of a fire that changed everything.

The questions remain unanswered. Why was such an object flown so low? What caused the radiation-like injuries? Who removed the road, and why?

Fire That Did Not Fade

The Cash–Landrum Incident stands apart from most unexplained encounters. It is not a story of distant lights or fleeting shadows. It is a story of heat you could feel, fire you could stand beneath, and damage that followed people for the rest of their lives.

Some mysteries fade into folklore. This one left scars, hospital records, and graves. It lingers like heat after flame—unseen, undeniable, and impossible to forget.

It reminds us that the greatest cost of secrecy is not confusion, but human lives, forever altered by something the world insists never burned at all.

Chapter 38

The man who faced two atom bombs

"One must imagine what it means to live after the end of the world—twice." — Albert Camus

An Ordinary Man

This is the story of Tsutomu Yamaguchi, an ordinary man who carried an extraordinary burden. It is not a tale of battlefield heroism, but of endurance. Not of victory, but of memory. He did not seek history, yet history found him—twice—at its most violent moment.

In the summer of 1945, Yamaguchi was a draftsman at Mitsubishi Heavy Industries, designing oil tankers. He was careful, methodical, and proud of his work. For three months, he had been away from home on assignment in Hiroshima. By early August, the job was finished. He was eager to return to his wife and infant son in Nagasaki.

A Small Turn That Saved a Life

On the morning of August 6, his bags were packed. As he walked toward the shipyard on the edge of Hiroshima, a small worry stopped him. He had forgotten his hanko, his personal name stamp. He turned back to retrieve it.

That small decision placed him just far enough away.

At 8:15 a.m., a distant sound reached the city. Yamaguchi looked up and saw a single American B-29 bomber high in the sky. A small object fell. A parachute opened. Then the world dissolved into white light.

The First Sun

The air ignited. The blast threw him into a potato field. He was less than two miles from the center of the explosion.

When consciousness returned, day had become night. A thick, black rain fell from the sky. His eardrums were ruptured. His face and arms were badly burned. The skin on his forearms hung loose, stripped by heat. The city he had walked through minutes earlier no longer existed. In its place were ash, fire, and voices crying for help.

He found coworkers who were still alive. Together they sheltered in a ruined air-raid bunker. The next day, walking through a landscape that felt unreal, he reached a train station that somehow still functioned. Wrapped in pain and disbelief, he boarded a train and traveled through the night back to Nagasaki.

Disbelief

On August 8, bandaged and shaking, Yamaguchi reported to his office at Mitsubishi. He tried to explain what had happened. He told them that a single bomb had destroyed an entire city.

His supervisor did not believe him.

"You're an engineer," the man said. "Calculate it. How could one bomb destroy a whole city?"

Yamaguchi had no calculation. He had only what his eyes had seen.

The Second Sun

The next day, August 9, at 11:02 a.m., he was still in that office. He was again describing Hiroshima, again trying to explain the impossible. As he gestured toward the Urakami district and said that a bomb like that could erase everything there, the world turned white once more.

The second sun rose over Nagasaki.

The windows exploded inward. Yamaguchi was thrown across the room. Behind him, a steel-reinforced stairwell absorbed the blast and saved his life. Again, he was within two miles of the center. Again, he survived.

What Remained Standing

In the days that followed, he searched desperately for his family. He found his wife, Hisako, and their infant son, Katsutoshi, alive. A ridge of hills had shielded their neighborhood. In a city of ruins, they held one another and endured.

Yamaguchi recovered slowly. His burns healed. His hair never grew back on one side of his head. Radiation sickness followed him quietly through life, a presence that never fully left. He returned to work. He raised his family. For decades, he spoke little about what he had witnessed.

A Voice Found Late

More than 160 people were later recognized by Japan as nijyuu hibakusha, survivors of both atomic bombings. In 2009, Tsutomu Yamaguchi was officially certified as the only person confirmed to have been present in both Hiroshima and Nagasaki at the exact moments of detonation.

Only late in life did he begin to speak openly. After losing his wife and son to cancers linked to radiation exposure, silence no longer felt possible. In his eighties, he wrote poetry and memoirs. In 2006, he traveled to the United Nations in New York.

He did not call himself lucky. He called himself "twice cursed."

"The reason that I hate the atomic bomb," he said, "is because of what it does to the dignity of human beings."

The Man Who Remembered

Tsutomu Yamaguchi died on January 4, 2010, at the age of ninety-three, from stomach cancer.

His life is more than a story of survival. It is a story of memory carried with care, of wounds that cannot be seen,

and of a man who stood beneath two suns and chose, for the rest of his long life, to speak for peace.

Chapter 39

The Lady of Fátima

"Where faith is deep, even the impossible is allowed to speak." — Blaise Pascal

Three Children and a Promise

In the spring of 1917, in a quiet hollow of stones and grass called Cova da Iria, near Fátima in Portugal, three children began a story that would outgrow them. They were shepherds, poor and uneducated, used to silence and open skies. Lúcia dos Santos was ten. Her cousins, Francisco Marto and Jacinta Marto, were nine and seven.

They said a lady appeared to them.

She was brighter than the sun, they said, yet gentle to look upon. She spoke softly of prayer, repentance, and suffering. She returned on the thirteenth day of each month, beginning in May. And she made a promise that would change everything: on October 13, 1917, she would perform a great miracle, so that all would believe.

Mockery, Fear, and Resolve

At first, the world laughed. Newspapers mocked the children. Officials accused them of lying or being manipulated. Priests were cautious. Local authorities interrogated them harshly. At one point, the children were detained and threatened with boiling oil if they did not deny their story.

They did not deny it.

As the months passed, something stirred across Portugal. The country was exhausted by poverty and grief. Europe was bleeding in the trenches of the First World War. People were hungry not only for bread, but for meaning.

Hope began to travel faster than doubt.

A Crowd Gathers

On the morning of October 13, people came.

They came walking for miles. They came in carts, on crutches, barefoot, and on their knees. Some came seeking healing. Some came to challenge the children. Some came simply because despair had driven them there.

By noon, nearly 70,000 people stood together in the open field. Farmers, skeptics, priests, journalists, scholars. The sky was dark. Cold rain soaked clothing and turned the ground to mud. No shelter. No comfort. Only waiting.

The children arrived.

At noon, Lúcia cried out that the lady was there. She said the war would end and that people must change their lives and pray.

Then the sky responded.

When the Sun Moved

According to thousands of witnesses, the clouds broke apart.

The sun appeared, not fierce, but pale—like a silver disc hanging low in the sky. Then it began to move.

It spun. It trembled. It seemed to rush toward the earth in a wild, zigzag motion. Light spilled across the field in waves of yellow, blue, and violet. Faces, clothes, and the muddy ground changed color again and again. For nearly ten minutes, the sun appeared to dance.

Fear swept through the crowd.

Many believed the end of the world had come. People fell into the mud, crying, confessing, begging forgiveness. Others stood frozen, unable to speak. Some later said their soaked clothes dried instantly. Others claimed their blindness lifted, their pain vanished.

And then, as suddenly as it began, the sun returned to its place.

The sky grew still.

Until They Saw

What makes that day difficult to dismiss is not only what was seen, but who saw it.

Avelino de Almeida, a known atheist and senior journalist for *O Século*, had gone to expose a fraud. Instead, he wrote a stunned, detailed account for one of Portugal's largest newspapers. The poet Afonso Lopes Vieira claimed to have seen the phenomenon from nearly twenty-five miles away. Doctors, lawyers, professors—people trained to doubt—added their testimonies.

They did not all agree on what it *meant*. But they agreed on what they had seen.

Between Heaven and the Human Mind

Later, scientists and skeptics searched for explanations. Some spoke of atmospheric effects, light bending through clouds, ice crystals, or optical illusions caused by staring at the sun. Others pointed to the power of expectation, to how shared belief and emotional intensity can shape perception.

None of these explanations erased the experience.

What happened at Fátima was not only in the sky. It was in thousands of minds at once—shaped by war, fear, hunger, faith, and longing. It was a moment where belief and perception met, and neither could fully explain the other.

What Remained

Fátima was never the same.

Francisco and Jacinta died soon after, during the influenza pandemic of 1918–1919, and were later canonized as saints. Lúcia became a Carmelite nun and lived until 2005, carrying the memory and the secrets she said were entrusted to her.

The Miracle of the Sun remains suspended between faith and psychology, devotion and doubt. To some, it is a divine sign. To others, a rare convergence of natural phenomena and human expectation. To history, it is both.

Even today, people return to that field in Portugal. They do not come only to look at the sky. They come to stand where hope once gathered in such force that, for a moment, the heavens themselves seemed to move.

And perhaps that is the quiet truth of that day: when enough human hearts lean in the same direction, even the sun feels invited to respond.

Bibiliography

American Psychiatric Association. DSM-5-TR: Diagnostic and Statistical Manual of Mental Disorders. APA Publishing, 2022.

Bartholomew, Robert E., and Simon Wessely. Mad Tales from the Raj: The European Insanity Epidemic in Colonial India. Routledge, 2002.

Canetti, Elias. Crowds and Power. Penguin Classics, 1960.

Carson, Rachel. Silent Spring. Houghton Mifflin, 1962.

Douglas, John, and Mark Olshaker. Mindhunter. Scribner, 1995.

Fromm, Erich. The Anatomy of Human Destructiveness. Holt, Rinehart and Winston, 1973.

James, William. The Varieties of Religious Experience. Harvard University Press.

Le Bon, Gustave. The Crowd: A Study of the Popular Mind. Dover Publications.

Matossian, Mary Kilbourne. Poisons of the Past: Molds, Epidemics, and History. Yale University Press, 1989.

McNeill, William H. Plagues and Peoples. Anchor Books, 1976.

Noll, Richard. Vampires, Werewolves, and Demons: Twentieth-Century Reports in the Psychiatric Liteature. Brunner/Mazel, 1992.

Snowden, Frank M. Epidemics and Society. Yale University Press, 2019.

Stone, Michael H. The Anatomy of Evil. Prometheus Books, 2009.

Tuchman, Barbara. A Distant Mirror: The Calamitous 14th Century. Ballantine Books, 1978.

Zimbardo, Philip. The Lucifer Effect. Random House, 2007.

ABOUT THE AUTHOR

Dr. Robin K. Mathew is a highly accomplished behavioral psychologist and ethnographer whose expertise is underpinned by extensive, global professional experience and cross-cultural engagement. His career reflects a deep appreciation for the complex socio-economic, ethnic, and linguistic variances shaping human experience, gained through direct interaction with individuals from nearly 90 different nationalities.

Dr. Mathew possesses a diverse and distinguished professional history, holding roles such as Research Assistant, Research Associate, Researcher, and Adjunct Faculty in prestigious international organizations. His multidisciplinary background includes formal education and experience in Information Technology, Human Resource Management, Psychology, Cyber Forensics, and Cyber Psychology.

He has contributed his expertise across various esteemed institutions, including the University of Toronto, University of Michigan, the Indian Institute of Management (IIM), ICFAI Business School, Best Buy, the Royal Bank of Canada, and Thomson Reuters. These roles have cultivated an unparalleled ability to synthesize insights across disciplines, significantly enriching his psychological analyses.

Over the past twelve years, Dr. Mathew has authored and published 22 books that delve deeply into facets of psychology and the human condition. Furthermore, he has contributed nearly 600 articles across a wide range of subjects, published in prestigious magazines both domestically and internationally. His prolific output captures the intricate nuances of human nature, informed by the vast knowledge accumulated throughout his professional journey.

Dr. Mathew is a Social Psychology Scientist currently working independently as an analyst for an international media agency.

Other books by the Author

Malayalam

1. Madamballiyille Manorogikal
2. Chekuthante Panipura
3. Chanakyante Kamukimar
4. Digital Nagavallimar
5. Cyber Parakaya Pravesham
6. Oru Kanyakayude Suvishesham
7. Jeevitha Vijyathinte Krithrima Thakkol
8. Kaanan Desham Thedi Poyavar

9. Geethanjali Voice
10. Raktham Viyarkkunna Kaikal
11.Oru Manashasthraknjanum Sancharikkatha Vazhikaliloode
12. Swargathinteyum Naragathinteyum Thelivukal

English
1. Lovers of Chanakya
2. In Quest of the Promised Land
3. I am Akira
4. The Expedition of Nun
5. The Artificial Key to Success
6. The Psychology of Mind Deception
7. Human Algorithm-Cyber Psychology for the Digital Age
8. The Grand Palace of Lucifer
9.The Saga of Nylari
10. The Proof of Heaven&Hell

Email: robinkmathew@gmail.com